INSIGHT POCKET GUIDES

Hong Kong

APA PUBLICATIONS
Part of the Langenscheidt Publishing Group

Hong Kong and Environs
4 km / 2.5 miles
CHINA
to Guangzhou
to Canton
to Shekou
to Macau
Deep Bay
Mirs Bay
NEW TERRITORIES
Tai Mo Shan 957
Kwai Tau Leng 486
Sharp Peak 468
Ma On Shan 702
Beacon Hill 452
Kowloon Peak 602
Castle Peak 583
Sunset Peak 869
Lantau Peak 933
Kowloon
HONG KONG
LANTAU
CHEK LAP KOK International Airport
Area: 1,097 sq. km.
Total number of Islands: 235
Population: 6.8 million
Climate: Subtropical
Terrain: Mountainous
Highest Peak: Tai Mo Shan, New Territories (958 metres)
National Flower: Bauhinia
KWANGTUNG PROVINCE
Canton
Pok Lo
Waichow
Ping Shan
Lung Kong
Siu Lam
Sun Wui
Suek Ki
Po On
Shum Chun
Hong Kong
Macau
South China Sea

Welcome!

Although a Special Administrative Region of China since 1997, much of Hong Kong remains unchanged. A typhoon shelter made good and surviving on its wits alone, Hong Kong continues to forge ahead despite economic and political difficulties thrown in its path. The Central district still has a slightly stuffy, formal bearing like it did in early colonial times; Tsim Sha Tsui and Causeway Bay are as frenetic as ever; Western and Yau Ma Tei retain their bygone Chinese flavours; Lantau, despite a new state-of-the-art airport, still has that lost-in-the-clouds aura; while Wan Chai is still the best party in Asia.

Author Joseph R Yogerst unravels Hong Kong with a series of carefully crafted itineraries spanning Hong Kong Island, Kowloon Peninsula, the New Territories and the Outlying Islands. This latest edition was updated by Hong Kong-based writer and editor Ann Galpin and her partner Jon Evans, who have carefully adapted Yogerst's original time-based itineraries to take in the latest developments in this city of perpetual change. Chapters on eating out, shopping, nightlife, a calendar of special events, and a practical information section complete this reader-friendly guide.

Joseph R Yogerst first visited Hong Kong in 1979 and recalls of that trip: 'To this day I can still remember what it was like to walk the crowded streets for the first time. Like any first-time visitor, I was overwhelmed by the assault of neon, tall buildings and earthy aromas that seem to escape from every turn that I took.' Later, he was offered an editorial position with a magazine and within a month was back on the plane, to live and work in Hong Kong for the next three years. In this book, Yogerst shares his easy familiarity with this exciting metropolis, Chinese in character, yet remarkably international in outlook.

C O N T E N T S

History & Culture

Day Itineraries

These full-day itineraries lead you to the city's essential sights, and include recommendations for lunch and dinner en route.

Pages 2/3: festive lights in Central District

Pick & Mix Itineraries

Eleven half-day itineraries explore selected aspects of this city in greater detail (1–4 are designed as morning tours, 5–8 are best done in the afternoons, and 9–11 are for the evenings).

Excursions

Pages 8/9: incense coils hanging from a temple roof

Eating Out, Nightlife & Shopping

Calendar of Special Events

Practical Information

Maps

HISTORY & CULTURE

It's easy to dismiss all of what transpired in Hong Kong prior to the unfurling of the first Union Jack. After all, wasn't it the British who created Hong Kong as we know it today? But ignoring the early stages of local history is a great mistake because they give even greater insight into the underlying forces that inspire Hong Kong today than anything that's happened since the arrival of Her Majesty's forces in 1841.

Hong Kong's frenzied construction is both a boon and bane to local archaeologists who are still searching for clues to early life along the south China coast. Much evidence has been destroyed in the march of progress, but at the same time bulldozers and earth movers have uncovered historical treasure troves that would have otherwise remained hidden. One of the best examples is the discovery in March 1992 of a 2,000-year-old village at Pak Mong with tools, weapons and pottery dating from the Western Han dynasty period (206BC–AD9) on the northwest shore of Lantau Island. The site was detected during the initial stages of construction of Hong Kong's new airport at Chek Lap Kok; and it may have remained buried for centuries if authorities had decided to build the airport somewhere else. Likewise, a four-chambered tomb structure dating

Early British sketches of Chinese merchants

from the middle of the Eastern Han dynasty (AD25–220) was discovered intact during preliminary work on the Eastern public housing project at Lei Cheng Uk on Kowloon peninsula in 1955.

Archaeologists have excavated a 5,000–6,000-year-old Stone Age settlement discovered at Tai Wan San Tsuen near Power Station beach on Lamma Island in early spring 1996. The artefacts uncovered substantiate earlier evidence that aborigines known as the Yueh people had flourished here for several thousand years before the Qin dynasty claimed the territory as part of the first Chinese empire in 214BC; while the Lei Cheng Uk and Pak Mong finds tell us that a sophisticated rural society similar to contemporary settlements elsewhere in southern China was thriving in Hong Kong at the time of the Roman Empire.

Collage of turn-of-the-century photos

Hong Kong must have remained a relative backwater for the next thousand years as nearby Canton (Guangzhou) began to prosper into a great trading city with connections to India, the Middle East and the rest of China. By AD900 pirates were operating in local waters, using the many islands and secluded coves as their lairs as they preyed on shipping in the Pearl River Delta. The Portuguese would later call them 'dwarf robbers' and for centuries they were a thorn in the side of imperial authorities in Canton. Among early pirate haunts were Cheung Chau Island and Chek Chue (Stanley) on the south coast of Hong Kong Island. Most of the pirates were wiped out by the 19th century, but small bands continued to plague the outlying areas of Hong Kong well into early years of the 20th century.

Meanwhile, the area that we now call the New Territories was undergoing its own transformation. Kublai Khan's Mongol hordes swept south into China destroying the Song dynasty and pushing gentry farmers south into areas beyond Mongol control. A clan called the Tangs settled in the fertile Shek Kong Valley where they established a cluster of walled villages called Kam Tin which endures to this day. Over the centuries, various other families settled in Hong Kong, the so-called 'Five Great Clans', for instance, who established semi-autonomous communities and brought civilisation to what had been an obscure part of China.

So the early settlers of Hong Kong were a mixed bag, a combination of pirates, fisherfolk and gentleman farmers. While they may have clashed at times, they had several things in common: they were largely free from imperial edict, removed from the royal court in Peking (Beijing) both in mind and body, used to getting things their own way and doing what they wanted without interference from higher authority. At the same time, they were an industrious lot who made a good livelihood off the meagre resources of the land, be it from planting or pilfering. And they have passed these traits down to their modern descendants, who tend to be proud and stubborn – seemingly at odds with the world – and at the same time terribly resourceful and self-reliant. You can claim that Hong Kong's economic miracle would have never happened without the British. But in the same breath you must give equal credit to the Hong Kong Chinese who believed in the potential of these scattered bits and bobs of land long before the Europeans.

Britain Claims the 'Barren Rock'

Portuguese navigator Jorge Alvares established contact with Cathay shortly after Vasco da Gama had rounded the Cape of Good Hope and 'discovered' India. By 1557 the Portuguese had established Macau. Hong Kong remained aloof from early interaction between Europe and China except for a fierce battle between Dutch and Portuguese fleets off the coast of Lantau at the turn of the 17th century.

Central District

The British were late to claim trading posts along China's coast. Captain James Weddell had no idea what he was starting when he led a small British fleet up the Pearl River in 1637. It was an ill-fated expedition that did not succeed in its goal of capturing Canton, but the skirmish was enough to send a chill up the spine of imperial China who called Weddell and his men 'the most ferocious of all the Western barbarians'. By the end of the century, British merchant ships were calling frequently on Canton. The voyages sparked a brief fascination with the Orient including construction of a pagoda at Kew Gardens and a rush to collect Ming vases.

In 1714, the British East India Company established a warehouse at Canton, and during the American Revolution the company began wholesale shipments of Indian opium to China in exchange for tea, silver and other precious goods. The British were by no means

19th-century harbour scene

the only opium traders, but they were by far the largest. China's hunger for this 'foreign mud' reached 2,000 chests by 1799, the year that the Qing imperial court in Peking banned its importation. Rather than forfeit massive profits, the British became ardent smugglers with the opium trade hitting £750,000 by 1816.

Relations between Britain and China were strained throughout much of the early 19th century. Events came to a head in 1839. The Qing emperor's newly-appointed Commissioner in Canton, Lin Tse-hsu, confiscated over 20,000 opium chests. The British felt compelled to protect the economic interests of her subjects and dispatched a naval expedition under Captain Charles Elliot to sort out the situation and establish a British base along the coast. Elliot chose Hong Kong Island near the mouth of the Pearl River because of its safe anchorage and easily defensible position and the Union Jack was planted at Possession Point on 26 January 1841. The annexation though didn't become official until the First Opium War ended the following year with the Treaty of Nanking.

A Second Opium War broke out in 1856 after an unprovoked military attack on a British ship in Chinese waters. This time, the British marched all the way to Peking to exact the Convention of Peking surrender treaty which included the outright cession of Kowloon peninsula and Stonecutters Island in 1860. Their toehold on the China coast was secure. The last chunk of real estate came in 1898 with the 99-year lease of the New Territories and 233 outlying islands from China.

An emblem of colonial Hong Kong

The Little Dragon is Born

Opium remained the foundation of British trade until the end of the 19th century when the powers that be in London began advising merchants that they should find something else to barter. By the outbreak of World War I – after just 62 years of British rule – Hong Kong's population had topped half a million. With the decline of the opium trade, local merchants turned to other items: tea, silk, gold and whatever else they could hawk to markets in Europe and North America. Hong Kong watched from the sidelines as China was engulfed by revolution, counter-revolution and then foreign invasion during the 1920s and 30s. She herself was invaded on 8 December 1941 when the Imperial Japanese Army poured across the border from already occupied southern China.

But the colony's economic miracle did not transpire until after World War II when a number of factors contributed to a dramatic transformation in Hong Kong's fortunes. The greatest factor was the 1949 Communist triumph in China, which sent millions of refugees – many of them wealthy – scrambling for safety in Hong Kong (and Taiwan). Some of them continued their journey to more distant points like America and Australia, but many stayed in Hong Kong and invested their money locally.

Then in 1951 the United Nations slapped a trade embargo on China for aiding North Korea in the Korean War (1950–53). Hong Kong went into shock at first, figuring that her days as an economic marvel were over. What would they do without trade? The answer was manufacturing. Small factories began to sprout in Kowloon and along the north shore of Hong Kong Island, many of them funded by refugees from Shanghai, and suddenly Hong Kong was able to export its own inexpensive goods to the rest of the world. The local manufacturing base continued to grow through the 1960s and 70s, as the financial and service sectors also took off.

Ferry piers in Aberdeen Harbour

But the 'golden age' didn't arrive until the late 1970s as China emerged from years of isolation and suddenly decided that it wanted to trade with the rest of the world again. Hong Kong was uniquely situated to funnel goods in and out of China, and act as a conduit of both tourism and investment.

1997: The Handover

The quintessential cerebral snapshot of post-1997 Hong Kong is the photo of the People's Liberation Army sentry outside the military headquarters in Admiralty. Ramrod stiff, immaculately turned out, the very model of a Chinese soldier but for the letters above his post which still read Prince of Wales Building!

As all the world knows, the Prince of Wales himself and Hong Kong's last British governor, Chris Patten, sailed off on the Royal Yacht in the early hours of 1 July 1997, ending an era that had seen Hong Kong transformed from an isolated speck on the map into the richest city on the coast of China. But amid all the propaganda and festivities was a real fear that life would change dramatically for the new Special Administrative Region's 6.8 million inhabitants.

On the surface, apart from some cosmetic changes – coins, stamps, flags – the regular tourist will see little that is very different from Hong Kong in the early 1990s. Queen Victoria's conspicuously unamused statue still sits in Causeway Bay. The MTR station north of Mong Kok is called Tai Chi in Chinese but Prince Edward in English. Nobody has changed the names of Possession Street, where the Union Jack was first raised in 1841, Queen's Road or any of thoroughfares named after prominent Britons/former governors.

Nathan Road at night

However, while Hong Kong functions under the late Deng Xiaoping's dictum of 'one country, two systems', the *Basic Law* (effectively a 'mini constitution') guarantees, on paper at least, the rule of law and a high degree of autonomy until 2047. Political opponents of the new regime have not hesitated to voice their doubts. The Provisional Legislature which came into being after the Handover was very much appointed by Beijing, while the elections held in May 1998 were slanted to make it more difficult for candidates who opposed Mainland policy. The first serious threat to the territory's judicial independence occurred in May 1999 when the Hong Kong government asked the National People's Congress in Beijing to overturn a ruling by the territory's highest court, the Court of Final Appeal, that would grant an estimated 1.67 million Mainland Chinese right of abode in Hong Kong. Nineteen Legislative Council members walked out in protest at the government's action. Hong Kong people watched all this with pursed lips, and got on with their own business. So the city is as glitzy, energetic and free-rolling as ever, but the question that hangs in sceptics' minds is whether Hong Kong is now more of a colony than it ever was under British rule.

Hong Kong Culture: Confucianism and Capitalism

Cynics like to snicker that the *only* culture in Hong Kong is capitalism. There is no denying that conspicuous consumption which peaked in the late 80s and early 90s is still rife. Rolls-Royces and Mercedes-Benz rule the roads. Mobile phones are considered necessities rather than luxuries. Parts of town just drip money, especially the residential Peak and the international designer stores of Central. And if there was a national sport, it would probably be gambling. Horseracing, the only legal form of gambling in Hong Kong outside of the Mark Six lottery, is the largest spectator sport and local punters bet in excess of US$6 billion a year – more than the gross national product of many Third World countries.

But Hong Kong's profligate days may be over. Uncertainty about the future after the transition of sovereignty has given way to deep concern over the unprecendented economic contraction of 1998 and the Asian economic crisis. In 1998 the government intervened in the stock market to fight off speculators and defend the Hong Kong dollar's peg against the US dollar; unemployment figures reached a 15-year high; and the territory suffered 60–70 percent decline in visitors from cash-strapped Japan and South Korea, traditionally two of its highest-spending tourist groups. The effects have been sobering and brought Hong Kong people back to more of their traditional values. People retain Confucian ideals and a strong work ethic.

Ancient Chinese customs are still observed. Buddhist and Taoist deities are actively worshipped in over 350 temples and religious festivals continue to outstrip their secular cousins in popularity. And when you're walking around Hong Kong, keep a sharp eye out for the small shrines to the animist earth gods and kitchen gods along the pavement or in the doorways of nearly every shop or restaurant. Hong Kong Chinese may enjoy the trinkets of modern life, but they have not lost touch with cultural roots that stretch back more than 4,000 years.

Historical Highlights

c4000BC Aborigines set up Stone Age settlements in coastal areas.
214BC Qin dynasty absorbs the territory and its indigenous Yueh people into first Chinese empire.
c1100 Mongol troops force farmers into southern China.
1277–9 Fleeing Song boy emperors find brief respite on Lantau and the Kowloon peninsula.
1521 Imperial troops expel unruly Portuguese traders from Tuen Mun.
1577 Portugal establishes official trading colony at Macau.
1662 Imperial edict aimed at quelling rebels and pirates forces coastal dwellers of San On province to uproot and move inland.
1669 Evacuation edict is reversed and coastal areas re-populated by Hakka people from northern China.
1714 Canton opened to foreign trade; British East India Company (EIC) establishes itself.
1773 The EIC unloads 150 pounds of Bengal opium at Canton.
1799 China bans opium trade but the drug continues to be smuggled.
1839 Commissioner Lin Tse-hu confiscates more than 20,000 chests of opium from British traders sparking off the First Opium War.
1841 Britain takes unofficial possession of Hong Kong Island after hoisting the Union Jack at Possession Point on 26 January.
1842 Hong Kong Island is officially ceded to Britain under the 'unequal' Treaty of Nanking.
1860 Kowloon Peninsula and Stonecutters Island are ceded to Britain as part of the Convention of Peking following the Second Opium War.
1898 Britain negotiates a 99-year lease of the New Territories and Outlying Islands.
1911 Qing dynasty falls; Sun Yatsen forms the Republic of China.
1938 Canton (Guangzhou) falls to Japan. Refugees who flee from across the border swell Hong Kong's population to 1.6 million.
1941 Japan enters World War II after bombing Pearl Harbour; Japanese forces simultaneously invade Hong Kong on Christmas Day.
1945 World War II ends and Hong Kong is liberated on 30 August. Population down to 600,000.
1949–50 Population swells to 2.2 million as Nationalists flee China following Communist victory.
1951 Trade embargo on China.
1954 Government initiates public housing programmes.
1966–7 Pro-Communists riots inspired by the Cultural Revolution in China shake Hong Kong.
1970 The first jumbo jet arrives at Kai Tak airport.
1975 Queen Elizabeth II becomes the first reigning British monarch to set foot in the colony.
1979 Mass Transit Railway opens.
1984 Margaret Thatcher and Chinese premier Zhao Ziyang sign a declaration that Hong Kong will revert to Chinese rule in 1997.
1987 Hong Kong Stock Exchange crashes.
1990 Beijing promulgates the Basic Law as blueprint for Hong Kong's constitution after 1997.
1992 Chris Patten takes over as the last British Governor.
1995 A fully-elected Legislative Council is voted into power as Patten's push for more democracy.
1996 Beijing's Preparatory Committee discuss appointment of 400-strong Selection Committee who will select first SAR chief executive and Provisional Legislature in 97.
1997 China resumes sovereignty, Tung Chee-hwa appointed Chief Executive and the Legco is replaced by Provisional Legislature.
1998 Elections held for Legco. Chek Lap Kok airport opens. The Hong Kong Stock Market dives on the back of the Asian economic crisis.
1999 The rule of law is undermined as government asks Beijing to overturn Court of Final Appeal's ruling on the right of abode.

Tai Wo Ping
to Shatin
Castle Peak Rd.
Ching Cheung Rd.
So Uk
Cornwall St.
Lai Chi Kok
Castle Peak Rd.
Cheung Sha Wan
Castle Peak Rd.
Shek Kip Mei
Kowloon Tong
Mei Foo
Sun Chuen
Chueng Sha Wan Rd.
Tai Po Rd.
Lai Chi Kok Rd.
Yau Yat
Tsuen
Waterloo Rd.
Sham Shui Po
Boundary St.
Boundary St.
Prince Edward Rd.W.
Ma Tau
Argyle St.
Tai Kok Tsui
Nathan Rd.
Mong
Kok
Waterloo Rd.
Fat Kwong St.
Kowloon
Ho Man
Yau Ma
Tei
Typhoon
Shelter
King's Park
to Tsuen Wan
Gascoigne Rd.
Jordan
Rd.
KCR Railway
Terminus
Nathan Rd.
Chatham Rd. S.
to Castle Peak Bay
KOWLOON
PARK
Western Harbour Crossing
to Macau
Tsim Sha
Tsui
Rd.
Salisbury
to Lantau, Lammat Cheung Chau
Airport Railway
Cross Harbour Tunnel
Sai Ying Pun
Connaught Rd. West
Victoria Harbour
Queens Rd. W.
Shek Tong
Tsui
Connaught Rd. Central
Chung Wan
(Central District)
Sheung Wan
University of
Hong Kong
Bun San Kui
(Mid-Levels)
Gloucester Rd.
Tung
Wan Chai
Hennessy Rd.
Victoria Peak
552
VICTORIA
PEAK
GARDEN
Queens Rd. E.
Racecourse

Hong Kong
500 m / 550 yards
Lung Cheung Rd.
Diamond Hill
Kowloon Peak
602
Wong Tai Sin
Choi Hung Rd.
San Po Kong
Prince Edward Rd. E.
Ngau Chi Wan
Choi Wan Estate
Clear Water Bay Rd.
Richland Garden
Kai Tak
Kai Yip Estate
Shun On Estate
Ngau Tau Kok
Sung Wong Toi Rd.
Telford Gardens
Kwun Tong Rd.
Jordan Valley
Sau Mau Ping
Ma Tau Kok
Crocodile Hill
Kowloon City Ferry Pier
To Kwa Wan
Tsui Ping Rd. Estate
Kwun Tong Rd.
Junk Bay Rd.
Kwun Tong Typhoon Shelter
Kwun Tong
Lam Tin
Kowloon Bay
Lei Yue Mun Rd.
Kwun Tong Ferry Pier
Yau Tong
Yau Tong Bay
North Point Ferry Pier
Eastern Harbour Tunnel
Island Eastern Corridor
Pak Kok (North Point)
Healthy Village Estate
King's Rd.
Sam Ka Tsuen Ferry Pier
Lei Yue Mun
Tsak Yue Chung (Quarry Bay)
Sai Wan Ho Ferry Pier
Sai Wan Ho
Shau Kei Wan Rd.
Tai Hang
HONG KONG ISLAND
Shau Kei Wan

Day Itineraries

The day itineraries are designed to give you a feel of Hong Kong's blend of modern urban energy and ancient Chinese mysticism, both of which combine to make this one of Asia's most exciting destinations. *Day 1* covers the heart of old British colonial Hong Kong, now the hub of business and banking. *Day 2* takes you to the mainland for a tour of Kowloon peninsula. *Day 3* explores the more tropical, relaxed side of Hong Kong on a journey across the southern bays of Hong Kong Island. The half-day tours that follow in the *Pick & Mix* section cover aspects of Hong Kong in greater detail, including a selection of evening tours covering nightlife. And when the city gets to you, the *Excursions* section are ideal for an experience of rural Hong Kong.

The Star Ferry plies a path across Victoria Harbour

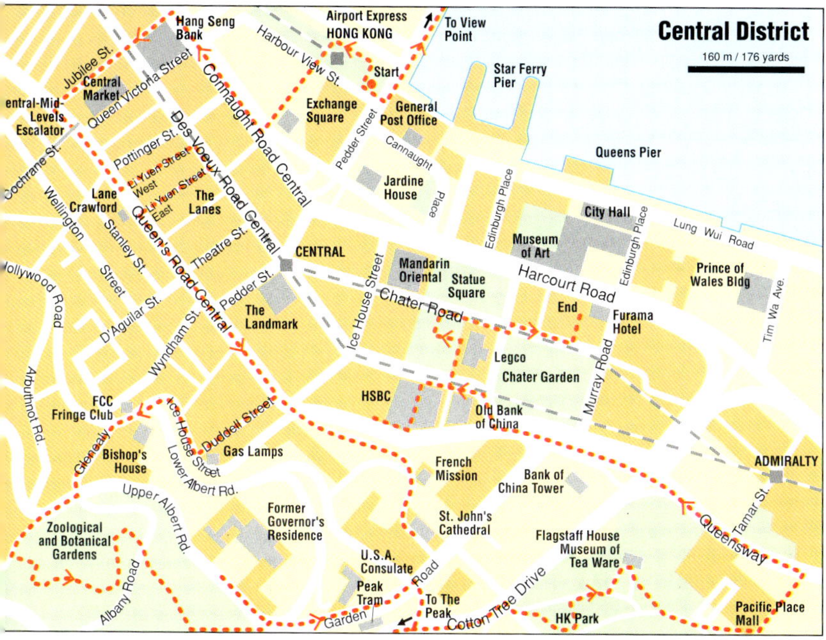

DAY 1

Hong Kong Island: Central District

Breakfast at a café in Exchange Square; explore Central district; St John's Cathedral; Zoological & Botanical Gardens; ride on the Peak Tram and lunch on the Peak; Hong Kong Park and the Flagstaff House Museum; by tram back to Central.

Your first day in Hong Kong is designed to give you a feel for the **Central District**, the hub of wealth and power in Hong Kong since the British first took possession of this barren rock on the coast of China in 1841. This is ideally a weekday itinerary; on Sundays and holidays thousands of smiling Filipino *amahs* (domestic helpers) gather on Central's sidewalks and squares, making for a festive atmosphere. As many of the buildings are roped off, getting past the crowds can be exhausting.

Start your day at **Hong Kong station** (Airport Express) Exit B2. Cross over Man Yiu Street, turn left and walk towards the green covered walkway leading to the Central Ferry Piers. On your right, you'll come to an open-air observation area, complete with power-

Bright lights, big city: Jardine House and Exchange Square

ful telescopes, where you can pause for panoramic views of **Victoria Harbour** and watch **Star Ferries** depart and dock at Central Star Ferry Pier. The green-and-white ferries are as much a part of the Hong Kong experience as bargain hunting or eating with chopsticks. The diesel-powered boats have been plying Victoria Harbour since 1898 and now carry more than 100,000 people each day.

Retrace your steps to Hong Kong station. If you require additional maps or tourist information, there is a **Hong Kong Tourist Information and Gift Centre** (Monday to Friday 9am–6pm, Saturday 9am–1pm) in the basement of porthole-studded Jardine House. Otherwise, take the glass elevator inside Hong Kong station to Level One and walk through the IFC Shopping Mall to **The Forum** at **Exchange Square**, where you can stop for breakfast or coffee at **Le Fauchon** (open from 7.30am Monday to Saturday; 10am on Sunday or holidays). The tinted glass and pink granite office complex of Exchange Square is home to the **Hong Kong Stock Exchange** (no visitors allowed). If you're early enough, you might see people practising *tai chi* around the powerful statue of a *Tai Chi Player* by Ju Ming, Dame Elizabeth Frink's *Water Buffalo*, the fountains and the Henry Moore sculpture on the Podium. Alternatively, if you're a cyber fan, you might prefer to take up the 10 minutes of free Internet time offered by the Pacific Coffee Company at Shop 1022 of the IFC Shopping Mall.

Follow the elevated walkway west beyond Three Exchange Square and turn left over Connaught Road where you see the sign for the hillside Escalator (symbol is a zigzagged mountain and man walking). This leads you through the Hang Seng Bank headquarters

Illegal buskers along Queen's Road

building, over Des Voeux Road and into **Central Market**. This is a 'stock exchange' of a much different sort: pigs, chickens, ducks, fish and other farm animals are sold here in profusion, as are fresh fruits and vegetables that are the foundation of Cantonese cuisine. Still at raised level, cross Queen's Road Central. The 800-metre **Central-Mid-Levels Escalator** (1993) runs down from the prime residential district of Mid-Levels from 6am to 10am and uphill from 10.20am to midnight. Return to street level by the short escalator on your left.

Queen's Road Central is a key shopping thoroughfare. The **CRC Department Store** on your immediate right sells all manner of products from mainland China. **Lane Crawford**, a couple of blocks east, is the oldest and one of most prestigious department stores in the city. As you head eastwards, notice the narrow alleys leading off to the sides. Steeply-stepped **Pottinger Street** to your right bustles with haberdashery and costume jewellery stalls. Souvenirs, leather and clothing bargains can be found down **The Lanes** of Li Yuen streets West and East to the left.

Continue east along Queen's Road Central and veer right up banyan-shaded Battery Path, past the elegant red-brick **Court of Final Appeal Building** (no visitors), dating from 1917 and also known as the **Former French Mission Building**, to **St John's Cathedral**. Dwarfed by the soaring cathedrals of commerce all around, this fine Victorian Gothic building was consecrated in 1849 and is believed to be the oldest Anglican church in the East. Pause for a moment to take in the peaceful interior with its turquoise timber ceiling and gently whirring fans.

Return to Queen's Road and take the second left into Duddell Street, scaling the stairs at the far end. The quaint gas lamps at the top and bottom of the steps are over 100 years old and are the only ones still in active service in Hong Kong. Follow the curve of **Ice**

A fresh fruit stall in Central

The Peak Tram has been toiling for more than 100 years

House Street past a cluster of old colonial buildings. Straight ahead is the **Dairy Farm Building** (1913), a red-brick structure that now houses the Foreign Correspondents' Club and Fringe Club. To the left is **Bishop's House** (1850) and **St Paul's Episcopal Church** (1911).

Head up Glenealy Street, veering right at the 'Ped Subway' sign and public toilets, through Glenealy subway. Turn left opposite the Caritas Canteen & Youth Centre into the **Hong Kong Zoological & Botanical Gardens** (open daily 6am–7pm). The zoo is small and old-fashioned by international standards but the gardens, established in 1864 and reached by a subway under Albert Road, offer a pleasant green retreat in the middle of the city.

Exit from the gardens eastern end and negotiate your way across the Upper Albert road 'spaghetti' junction by two flights of steps. You can detour left along Upper Albert Road to view the front of the former **Governor's Residence** through the wrought-iron gates (no visitors allowed) or go down Garden Road. Follow the signs to Hong Kong Park across the road just after the **Helena May** ladies' club (1916) on your right, bringing you to the **Peak Tram** station.

In continuous operation since 1888, the funicular tramway was built to serve the wealthy residents of the Peak who previously had to rely on human-carried sedan chairs for transport to the waterfront. Trams depart every 10 to 15 minutes from 7am to midnight for a breathtaking journey to the summit. The panoramic views from the top are magnificent on a clear day. There are lots of entertainment and dining options at the **Peak Tower** or stop for lunch at **Café Deco** in the Peak Galleria or the quaint **Peak Café** (1901), just across the road (see *Itinerary 7: Victoria Peak Walk*).

Descend on the Peak Tram and turn right under the Cotton Tree Drive flyover into **Hong Kong Park** (open daily 6.30am–11pm).

Wander round the high-tech aviary and greenhouses, see couples posing for photos in full wedding regalia by the registry office, or climb the 105 steps of the observatory tower for another sweeping view. But the primary reason to come here is the **Flagstaff House Museum of Tea Ware** (open daily except Wednesday 10am–5pm). Built in 1846, the house is the oldest European structure still standing in Hong Kong. It served as the residence of the Commander-in-Chief of the British Forces for more than 130 years.

Leave the park by the Supreme Court exit. Take the elevator on your left down to **Pacific Place**, a huge hotel and shopping complex. If you're not in a shopping mood, follow the signs for the Admiralty/MTR/Queensway Plaza, reached via a pedestrian bridge over Queensway. Half way across, take the steps down to the tramway and ride two stops on a westbound tram.

The first stop takes you as far as the **Bank of China** (1989), a spectacular prism-like structure designed by Chinese-American architect I M Pei and, at 70 storeys (367.4m), the second tallest in town. **Chater Garden**, opposite, once home of the exclusive Hong Kong Cricket Club is now a pleasant urban green space. The tramline wraps around the art deco-style old **Bank of China Building** (1950) before stopping outside the futuristic **Hongkong Bank** (HSBC) headquarters building (1985). Designed by British architect Sir Norman Foster, it is considered to be one of the world's most innovative modern structures. Walk beneath the building and gaze up at its 'guts' through the glass floor. Take the escalator up to the main hall during banking hours for a closer inspection.

HSBC Building

Cross Des Voeux Road to see the domed **Supreme Court** building (1912). Designed by the architects responsible for the Buckingham Palace facade and the Victoria & Albert Museum in London, this is now home to Hong Kong's Legislative Council and known as the **Legco Building** (Legco sittings are open to the public by prior reservation, tel: 2869 9399).

From here it is an easy stroll to the Star Ferry via **Statue Square**. The south section houses a statue of Sir Thomas Jackson, an early doyen of the Hongkong Bank while the north side is dominated by a cenotaph to the war heros and the members-only Hong Kong Club. Or end the day on a high note by watching the city light up over dinner at **La Ronda** revolving restaurant (tel: 2848 7422; dinner buffet 6.30–10.30pm) at the top of Hotel Furama.

DAY 2

Kowloon: Tsim Sha Tsui District

Ocean Terminal; Cultural Centre; Museum of Art; Space Museum; The Peninsula Hotel; Nathan Road; Signal Hill; Kowloon Park; Science Museum; Hong Kong Museum of History; Granville Road's 'factory outlets' and Harbour City.

The following walking tour is designed to help you get your bearings around **Tsim Sha Tsui**, the bustling down-town district on the tip of **Kowloon** peninsula. It is famous for its museums, hotels, restaurants, shopping and entertainment venues. Start from Kowloon's **Star Ferry concourse**. The adjacent pier, **Ocean Terminal**, is where international cruise ships berth, an impressive sight if the QE2 or one of the other enormous liners is in town.

Just to the east stands a 45m (147ft) tall brick-and-stone **clock tower** (1916). This is all that remains of the grand Kowloon-Canton Railway Terminus where once you could hop on a train to go all the way to Paris. The Edwardian station was demolished in 1978 to make way for the sweeping curves of the **Hong Kong Cultural Centre** (1989); you can still make the journey from the modern terminus in Hung Hom, but somehow the glamour has gone.

Take the spiral staircase near the clock tower up to the elevated

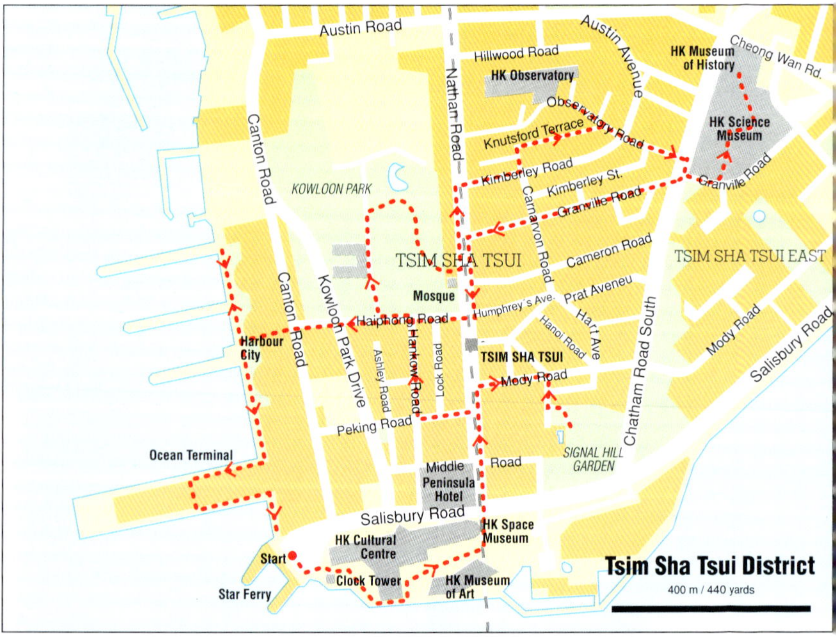

Nathan Road is always a treat for the eyes – and pocket book

promenade and observation gallery. The waterfront here offers such magnificent vistas of Hong Kong Island that it's hard to figure out what inspired the architect to design a windowless façade for the Cultural Centre. Aesthetics aside, the building is Hong Kong's premier venue for classical music, ballet and theatre. It is home base to the HK Philharmonic and HK Chinese orchestras, and attracts top performers from the international circuit as well as local musicians. Take the entrance opposite César's *Flying Frenchman* sculpture to check if there are any performances you'd like to see.

Walk through the Cultural Centre to the **Hong Kong Museum of Art** (Friday to Wednesday 10am–6pm, Sunday 1–6pm). The museum has collections of Chinese antiquities, paintings and calligraphy, and contemporary Hong Kong art, but most visitors are drawn by the fascinating pictures of old Hong Kong, Canton and Macau on the third floor.

The large white egg-shaped dome just beyond is the **Hong Kong Space Museum** (tel: 2734 2722; Monday, Wednesday to Friday 1–9pm, Saturday, Sunday and some holidays 10am–9pm; closed Tuesday and some holidays; admission fee), a high-tech planetarium with wide-screen Omnimax-film and Sky shows; a must-see for space enthusiasts both young and old.

Directly across Salisbury Road is **The Peninsula**, the grand dame of Hong Kong hotels and first choice for visiting celebrities and heads of state since it opened in 1928. A 30-storey extension tower, crowned with a Philippe Starck-designed restaurant and private heli-pad, means that Hong Kong's only historic hotel is also its most technologically advanced. However, it is the beautifully restored **Peninsula Lobby**, without a doubt Hong Kong's most elegant gathering place, that wins most visitors' hearts. In recognition of this, the dress code has been relaxed until 6.30pm, making it a

Cathay Pacific's first plane hangs inside the Science Museum

wonderfully atmospheric place to stop for morning tea or coffee. Exit via the Peninsula Shopping Arcade onto bustling **Nathan Road**, a canyon of neon lined with hotels, restaurants and shops, also dubbed Kowloon's 'Golden Mile'.

Walk north to the Peking Road junction. For an optional detour, cross Nathan Road and walk half a block north, turning right into Mody Road and right again into Minden Row. This brings you to **Signal Hill Garden**, a little oasis of calm and greenery which sadly, is likely to be affected by an underground extension to the Kowloon-Canton Railway some time in 2000. At the summit you'll find **Blackhead Signal Tower** (open daily 9–11am and 4–6pm) which was built in 1907 to house the time-ball by which ships in the harbour adjusted their chronometers before the days of radio signals. Retrace your steps to Peking Road.

Walk west along Peking Road and turn north into **Hankow Road**. This is the heart of the old sailor bar district. However, the biggest crowd-puller these days is the HMV mega-store, opposite, with the largest collection of CDs in Hong Kong. Continue north along Hankow Road and cross Haiphong Road to the south entrance of **Kowloon Park** (open daily 6am–midnight). Occupying the site of a former British military barracks, the park is a breath of fresh air for nearby residents and office workers, with lakes, ornamental gardens, aviaries and a sports complex. Art lovers will enjoy the open-air **Sculpture Walk**.

Leave the park by the entrance beside **Kowloon Mosque**, Hong Kong's largest mosque, with a white marble dome and minarets. Cross Nathan Road and walk north to the crenellated Victorian gothic-style building at No 136. Set back from the road up a double flight of steps, this was the former Kowloon-British School (1902) and now houses the **Heritage Resource Centre** of the Antiquities and Monuments Office (tel: 2721 2326; Monday, Wednesday to Friday 9.30am–5pm, weekends and some holidays 9.30am–1pm, closed Tuesday and some holidays).

Retrace your steps down Nathan Road and turn left into Kimberley Road. Tucked away up a set of steps opposite the turning to Carnarvon Road is **Knutsford Terrace**, an ideal place for lunch.

After lunch, continue east along Knutsford Terrace onto Observatory Road. Another of Hong Kong's colonial buildings, the **Hong Kong Observatory** (arrange for visits at tel: 2721 2326).

Kowloon light show

Head east along Observatory Road to the junction with **Chatham Road South**, which marked the original waterfront prior to the huge reclamation that now forms Tsim Sha Tsui East. Turn right and cross Chatham Road South by the raised pedestrian walkway at the entrance to Granville Road. Follow the signs to the **Hong Kong Science Museum** (tel: 2732 3232; Tuesday to Friday 1–9pm; weekends and some holidays 10am–9pm; closed Monday and some holidays; admission fee except for Wednesday) a wonderland of interactive, hands-on exhibits exploring the mysteries of science and technology. Next-door at No 100 is the **Hong Kong Museum of History** (tel: 2724 9042; Monday to Thursday, Saturday 10am–8pm; Sunday and some holidays 1–8pm; closed Friday and some holidays). The museum's permanent exhibition, scheduled to open in 2000, will trace the evolution of Hong Kong from a peaceful rural backwater to a teeming metropolis.

Head back over Chatham Road and west along **Granville Road**, famous for its 'factory outlet' shops selling 'seconds' or over-runs of garments manufactured locally for export.

Granville Road takes you back to Nathan Road, the heart of Tsim Sha Tsui. Head south to the crossing by Humphrey's Road and turn right down Haiphong Road to Canton Road. Straight ahead is the gargantuan **Harbour City** complex, a maze of hotels and interconnecting shopping malls stretching nearly the entire length of **Canton Road**. To end the day, head back to the Peninsula for cocktails at **Felix**, or mingle with the stars in **Planet Hollywood** at Canton Road.

Harbour City: five interconnecting malls for the price of one

Jaws

Hong Kong Island: South Side

Aberdeen Harbour, Ocean Park and Middle Kingdom, Repulse Bay, Stanley village and market.

The south side of Hong Kong Island offers a refreshing break from the intense urbanisation of the north shore. Its four main attractions – Aberdeen Harbour, Ocean Park, Repulse Bay and Stanley – are easily accessible by bus. The journey is part of the fun as there are some breathtaking views along the winding coastal road; best enjoyed from upstairs on the double-deckers. It's more relaxing to explore the south side – especially Ocean Park – on a weekday as Hong Kongers flock here in droves on weekends and holidays.

Start this tour in Central by hopping on a No 7 or No 71 bus to Aberdeen at either the open-air bus station in front of the Central Ferry Piers or outside the Hang Seng Bank headquarters building on Connaught Road. The route takes you round the west coast of the island via Western district and Pokfulam.

Leave the bus on Aberdeen Main Road outside the Hongkong Bank (HSBC) for a stroll along Aberdeen waterfront to soak in the atmosphere of Hong Kong's liveliest waterway.

Aberdeen has been a fishing port for hundreds of years, long before the British decided to name it after their Foreign Secretary, Lord Aberdeen, in the 1840s. Its Chinese name, Heung Kong Tsai (Little Fragrant Harbour), is thought to allude to the port's cen-

Aberdeen Harbour in the misty morning light

Killer show at Ocean Park

turies-old trade in fragrant incense wood. At one time more than 20,000 Tanka and Hoklo 'boat people' lived on traditional wooden junks in the sheltered anchorage. The majority have traded their floating homes for high-rise flats nearby, but a sizeable seaborne community remains; a sampan ride through this crowded waterway is a memorable highlight of any visit. The sampan operators (often surprisingly elderly women) keep an eye out for tourists and are always happy to negotiate a fee for a quick and occasionally rather hair-raising spin between the fishing trawlers, ramshackle live-aboard junks and upmarket yachts and pleasure craft, rounded off by three resplendently gaudy floating restaurants.

Palatial in size and unrestrainedly theatrical in decor, the **Jumbo Floating Restaurant** and sister establishments are an attraction in their own right. If you're feeling peckish, you can forsake the sampan-ride and still enjoy a trip through the harbour by taking one of their free shuttle boats over to try out a few *dim sum* dishes.

The next stop depends on your priorities. You can either proceed straight to Repulse Bay, or spend the rest of the morning at nearby Ocean Park. Both can be reached by taking a bus from Aberdeen Main Road; for Repulse Bay take the No 73 from outside the Liu Chong Hing Bank and for Ocean Park take the No 48 from outside the Hongkong Bank (HSBC) or the No 170 from outside the Liu Chong Hing Bank. Alternatively, take a taxi there.

Ocean Park (open daily 10am–6pm; admission fee) attracts over three million visitors a year and is billed as Southeast Asia's largest amusement and entertainment centre. The oceanariums and spectacular cliff-top setting make it worth visiting even if theme parks usually turn you cold. Highlights include the stunning **Atoll Reef** and **Shark Aquarium**; 360 degree views from the 72-m (236-ft) observation tower; cable car and escalator rides up and down the headland; the **Raging River** and other hair-raising adventure rides; and **Middle Kingdom** which traces 5,000 years of Chinese history through cultural shows, artisan workshops and architectural reproductions. The most recent additions are two giant pandas, An An and Jia Jia, a gift from the Beijing government, who reside in HK$80 million air-conditioned habitat. Allow at least four hours to get round the main attractions, longer if you're with children or if it's a weekend or holiday.

To continue on to **Repulse Bay**, turn right out of Ocean Park Main Entry Plaza, walk through the carpark, cross Wong Chuk Hang Road, head left to the bus-stop and hop on a southbound No 73, 6A or 260 bus, which travels past Deep Water Bay, the exclusive Hong Kong Golf Club and Royal Hong Kong Yacht Club's

The Verandah restaurant, a reproduction of the old Repulse Bay Hotel

base on Middle Island (both clubs are members-only).

Repulse Bay is one of the more picturesque and popular beaches in Hong Kong. It's hard to find a spare inch of sand on summer weekends and holidays, but it's often deserted on weekdays. Villas of wealthy colonial residents once surrounded the bay, but nowadays Miami-style condominium blocks dominate the backdrop. At the south end of the beach is the rather bizarre **Life Guard Club** with temple-esque features and a whimsical collection of images, including huge statues of the Buddhist goddess Kwun Yam and her Taoist counterpart Tin Hau, both protectors of fishermen.

There are lunch choices to suit every pocket here. If you're feeling like a splurge, head for the romantic **Verandah** restaurant (tel: 2315 3166) in the Edwardian-style building at 109 Repulse Bay Road. The structure is a recreation of the old Repulse Bay Hotel (1920), the belle of colonial society between the wars. The original was pulled down in 1982 to make way for the massive wall of condos behind. Then the developers had pangs of guilt and decided to rebuild it according to its original plans! Managed by the Peninsula hotel group, the Verandah is justifiably popular and advance bookings are recommended at weekends. It's sister establishment Hei Fung Terrace (tel: 2812 2622) offers exquisite *dim sum*. If you're feeling under-dressed, pick up a snack at one of the fast-food outlets on Beach Road.

Once you've had your fill of the beach, catch a No 6, 6A, 73 or 260 bus to Stanley. The route hugs picturesque coastline of **Chung Hom Wan** (bay)

Song birds at Stanley Market

looking westward to Lamma Island. Like Aberdeen, **Stanley** was a thriving fishing village long before the British arrived. The local Hakka people named it Chek Chue or 'robbers' lair' because it was a haven for smugglers and pirates. Nowadays, it's a popular residential enclave for wealthy commuters, with a seaside village atmosphere, a number of fine restaurants, and, of course, its famous street market.

Stanley Market consists of a maze of stalls and little shops, just down the hill from the bus stop on Stanley Village Road. Apart from the colourful fresh food and flower section, it caters largely to tourists and expats. Although prices are no longer a 'steal', it's still a great place to browse around for presents and souvenirs. Good buys include beautifully embroidered household linens, silk fashions, and craft items from China and southeast Asia.

Beyond the strip of bars and restaurants on Stanley Main Street is a tiny **Tai Wong Temple** built into a rock. Further north, is a **Tin Hau Temple**, dedicated to the Goddess of Heaven and protector of sea-farers. Inside is an ancient drum and bell dated 1767, it belonged to the legendary Qing dynasty pirate chief Cheung Po-Tsai, and a rather tatty skin of a tiger shot here in 1942. The temple used to be on the seashore but recent reclamation has left it surrounded by a modern housing development. This is at least partially compensated by the reconstruction of **Murray House**, a colonial military barracks dating from 1843 which was knocked down in 1982 to make way for the Bank of China tower in Central. Its new incarnation as a complex of trendy bars and restaurants is scheduled to open in early 2000.

Stanley sales pitch

In the opposite direction, down Wong Ma Kok Road, is secluded **St Stephen's Beach**, one of the most beautiful strands in Hong Kong, and **Stanley Military Cemetery**, where early colonial soldiers and World War II POW's (including the American consul to Hong Kong) are buried.

Back on **Stanley Village Road**, at No 88, the former Stanley Police Station (1859), the territory's oldest police building, is now an expensive restaurant. Watch the sunset over Stanley Bay and dine in one of the restaurants on Stanley Main Street. Book ahead to secure a table with a view at Stanley's French (tel: 2813 8873) or Stanley's Oriental (tel: 2813 9988) both at No 90B. To return to Central, hop on a No 6, 6A, 6X or 260 bus; if your next destination is Tsim Sha Tsui or Kowloon, you can take the No 973.

Pick & Mix

Morning Itineraries

1. Western District

Hong Kong University; the old residential and trading district of Sai Ying Pun; Western Market; and Luk Yu Tea House.

Start the day on a cultural note with a visit to the peaceful campus and art gallery of **Hong Kong University** (HKU), at the western end of Bonham Road. Get there by taxi, or hop on a No 3B bus from the bus stop in front of Jardine House on Connaught Road in Central. Ask for *dai hok* ('big school') if the driver doesn't speak English. Get off just past the University Museum and Art Gallery on your left at 94 Bonham Road.

HKU has expanded out of all recognition since a grand total of 72 students enrolled for the first intake in 1912. The original building – a stately Edwardian structure with internal courtyards and fountains – still stands at the top of the sloped driveway; it now houses the Arts Faculty. The graceful **Hung Hing Ying Build-**

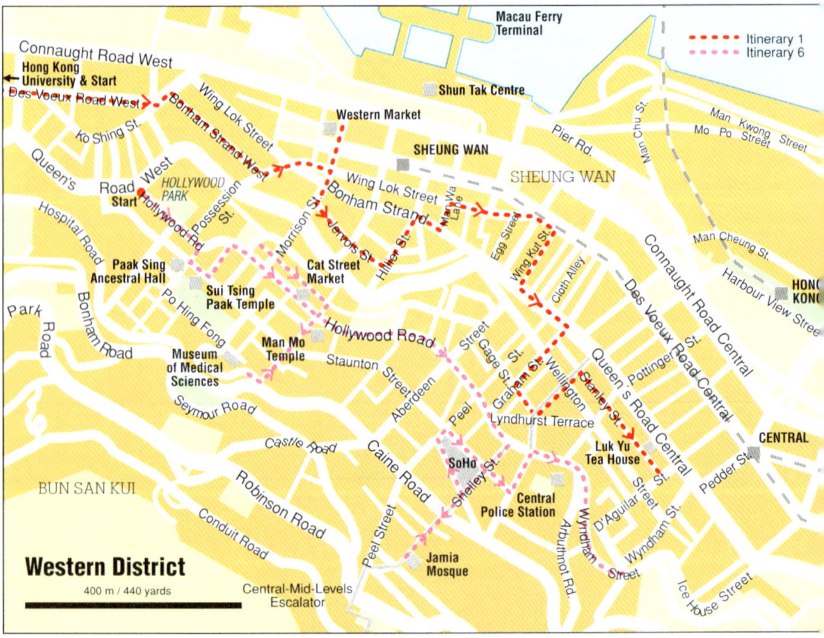

ing (not open to the public) opposite was built in 1919 and today houses the Music Department. Don't only expect to see students and lecturers; the campus is a popular venue for fashion shoots and wedding photos.

Wander back down the driveway to the **University Museum & Art Gallery** (tel: 2975 5600; open Monday to Thursday and Saturday 9.30am–6pm; Sunday and some holidays 1.30–5.30pm). The 1930s **Fung Ping Shan Building** houses an interesting collection of early Chinese bronzeware and ceramics, a unique group of Nestorian crosses, and some fine late Ming and early Qing paintings; contemporary art is exhibited in the adjoining **T T Tsui Building**.

Continue east along Bonham Road and turn left down **Centre Street**. The section below High Street retains a flavour of an older Hong Kong. As you head east along **High Street**, notice the small earth god shrines outside each shop, and the protective deity's altar inside the metal workshop at No 47.

The junction with **Eastern Street** has lost most of its former colonial charm since all but the classical façade of the 1892 hospital building (originally a home for European nurses) was demolished to make way for new development and the handsome redbrick colonial building beside it was converted into a methadone clinic. However, the magnificent banyan trees shading Eastern Street still hint at a bygone elegance.

Continue down Eastern Street and turn right along **Queen's Road West** till you reach a row of shops on the right, selling floral wreaths, joss sticks, paper offerings and brass urns. If you haven't guessed already, these are boutiques for the deceased. Everything you need for a traditional Chinese funeral can be found here; the coffin shops are just round the corner on Hollywood Road. Keeping up with the times, paper items for the afterlife now include speed-boats, planes, microwave ovens, rice-cookers, mobile phones, karaoke disc-players, etc.

Cross Queen's Road West and cut down **Li Sing Street** (also signed Li Ying Street) through to **Des Voeux Road West**. Turn right and browse your way past the shops selling traditional Chinese medicines and dried food. To the uninitiated, the aromas can seem rather pungent but the displays of the exotic dried ingredients used in authentic Chinese cuisine are fascinating.

Continue on Des Voeux Road West until you reach **Bonham Strand West** on your right. The shops here deal in the wholesale trade of ginseng, antelope horn, sharks' fin, birds' nests,

A regular market stall holder

Façade of the restored Western Market

abalone and other exotic produce prized in traditional Chinese medicine or cooking.

At the end, bear left round to **Morrison Street** and head harbour-wards to the **Western Market** (1906). Used as a fresh produce market for more than 80 years, the handsome red-brick building was sensitively restored and re-opened in 1991 as a period shopping mall. You'll find interesting memorabilia, handicrafts, toys and other gift items on the ground floor, and fabric merchants selling everything from Chinese silk to Harris tweed upstairs. Prices are fair and the merchants know their stuff; they moved here when the legendary 'Cloth Alley' bazaar on Wing On Street was closed down to make way for high-rise office towers. If you're thirsty, take a break in Six Bugs Antiques & Café on the ground floor.

Refreshed, head back up Morrison Street away from the harbour. The **Urban Council Sheung Wan** civic complex on the right houses one of the biggest public food markets in Hong Kong; the building's no picture but there's a lot of atmosphere inside. Turn left down **Jervois Street**, which marked the waterfront until the first harbour reclamation began in 1852. The Yuen Mau Hing Kee Tea Co at No 99–101 has some great terracotta teapots. Traditional cooking implements are still produced in artisan workshops down the side-streets; one shop you shouldn't miss is **No 13 Hillier Street**. The geckos and snakes in the cages near the dark entrance are no illusion. This is one of Hong Kong's fabled snake shops; concocting soup, wine, and other traditional recipes from snakes and other reptiles. Snakes are considered

Slurping snake soup

Chinese dried goods stall

a winter-time 'delicacy' as the meat and body fluids are believed to fortify the human body against cold; geckos are apparently on the menu all the year round.

Head north up Hillier Street and turn right into Bonham Strand, which lost its harbour-front position after a second reclamation scheme was completed in 1904. Turn left at the Hongkong Bank (HSBC) into **Man Wa Lane**, familiarly known as '**Chop Alley**', where dozens of chop makers ply their wares. A 'chop' is a Chinese seal carved from natural materials like jade, soapstone, bone and ivory. There have been chop makers here since the 1920s; the art itself is some 3,000 years old. You can have the proprietor translate your name for a custom-made seal. It takes one to four hours to carve the characters.

Head east along Wing Lok Street, turning right on Des Voeux Road and right again down **Wing Kut Street**, a chance survivor of the lively alley markets that once characterised this area. Turn left into **Queen's Road Central**. On your left at No 151, the Ying Kee Tea Co sells attractive metal tea caddies and traditional 'cakes' of Chinese tea. Opposite at No 152 is the Eu Yan Sang Medical Hall, one of the most venerable Chinese pharmacies in town (for some strange reason complete with a medieval knight on horseback in the front window). It's worth a visit as the displays of exotic remedies are labelled in English as well as Chinese.

Your curiosity sated, turn right up **Graham Street** with its bustling fresh vegetable and meat stalls, left into Gage Street and left again onto **Cochrane Street**, where the Dublin Jack offers tasty pub food and liquid refreshments. For a more traditional Hong Kong experience, continue on down beside the Central-Mid-Levels Escalator and turn right into **Stanley Street** to enjoy *dim sum* and piping hot tea at the legendary **Luk Yu Tea House** (No 24–26). This is one of the few old-style tea houses left. Don't be put off by the sometimes rather brusque service or the racket; the noise is part and parcel of the authentic tea house experience. Expect to pay HK$100–150 a head. You might also like to shop for some portable nostalgia at the Sun Chau Book & Antique (No 32).

2. Causeway Bay

Explore the older and greener sides of this shopping mecca.

Crowded with shopping malls, department stores and restaurants, **Causeway Bay** is a veritable consumer paradise. This itinerary explores some of its other attractions, starting with a stroll through the city's largest urban greenspace, **Victoria Park**. The park is at its best in the early morning when hundreds of *tai chi* devotees gather to practise their graceful exercises. To get there, take a taxi to the Park Lane Hotel, or the MTR to Causeway Bay (Exit E) and head two blocks east along Great George Street.

Make your way to the park's northwest corner and take the pedestrian bridge over congested Victoria Park Road highway for a panoramic view of **Kowloon** and the **Causeway Bay Typhoon Shelter**. The shelter houses a mixed bag of pleasure boats (the Royal Hong Kong Yacht Club is on the headland to your left), rickety wooden junks and sampans. A sizeable community still lives on the boats so there's lots of activity in the morning as family members commute to work and school by sampan.

In a small garden just west of the footbridge is the **Noon Day Gun**, immortalised by Nöel Coward in the song *Mad Dogs and Englishmen*. The practice of firing a cannon at the stroke of noon was begun by Jardine, Matheson & Co in the 1840s when they set up their trading base on the Causeway Bay waterfront (then considerably inland from its present location). Jardine has long since moved to Central but continue to operate the salute, a quaint anachronism and daily reminder of the area's colourful trading history.

Back in Victoria Park, follow the main west-east path to the fork halfway across and bear right to the exit on the southeast corner; if

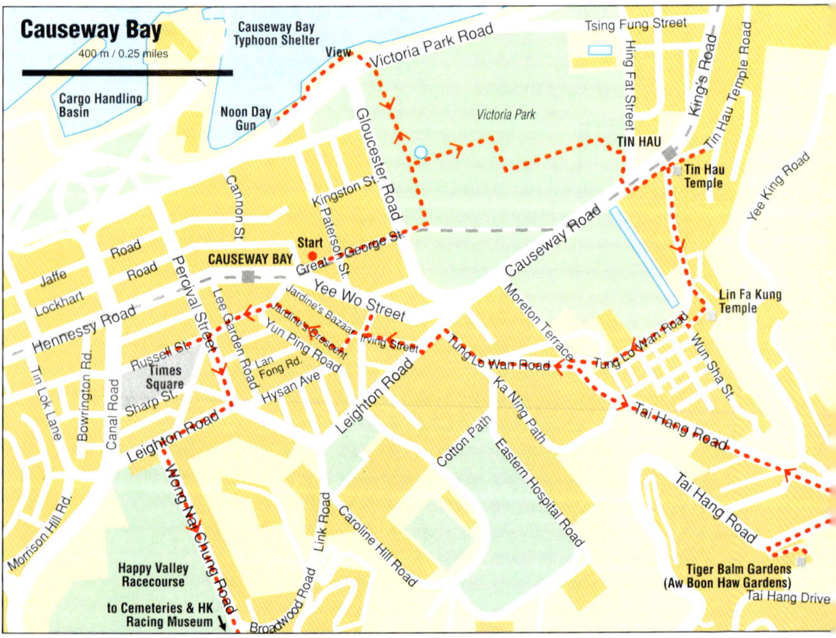

Junks and pleasure boats share Causeway Bay

you miss the fork and end up at the fire-station, take a right turn down to the same point. Cross Causeway Road, and turn left over Tung Lo Wan Road and up the short rise to the **Tin Hau Temple**, perched on a granite ledge that once looked out over the bay. The Taoist Queen of Heaven and protector of sea-farers, Tin Hau has a huge following, with numerous temples all over Hong Kong. This particular temple dates from the 18th-century; it has exquisite decorative details and shrines to the Azure Dragon and White Tiger beyond the moongates in the covered courtyard.

Retrace your steps down Tin Hau Temple Road, turn left into Tung Lo Wan Road for three blocks to **Lin Fa Kung Temple** (open daily 7am–5pm), set back down a lane of the same name. Dating back to 1864, but renovated in early 1999, the temple is dedicated to the Goddess of Mercy. It consists of an octagonal structure in front and straddles a giant boulder to the rear, making it one of Hong Kong's most unusual Buddhist shrines.

Inside, the main shrine is covered in blinking fairy-lights, and there's a large bronze urn and a turtle pool beyond the door opposite the entrance. Take the internal wooden staircase to the upper level, where you should be able to make out the shadowy silhouette of a dragon on the ceiling through the incense fumes; this may be a reference to the weird and wonderful Fire Dragon dance in which 100 men support a 'dragon' made of smoking joss sticks through the streets during the annual Mid-Autumn Festival.

From here, continue along Tung Lo Wan Road for an-

Causeway Bay's Tin Hau Temple

Chinese mythology at Tiger Balm Gardens

other five blocks. This road was once on the original waterfront and its name Tung Lo Wan (Copper Gong Bay) is also the Chinese name for Causeway Bay. Scale the stairs opposite the bus station and take a No 11 bus up the steep Tai Hang Road to the **Aw Boon Haw (Tiger Balm) Gardens** (open daily 9.30am– 4pm).

Built in 1935 by the millionaire philanthropist Aw Boon Haw, who made his fortune with the Tiger Balm ointment, the gardens are filled with garish statues and bas-reliefs depicting events from Chinese mythology. There's a good view from the Tiger Pagoda. The gardens have been under threat of redevelopment since early 1999, so it might be worth checking if they're still open before you visit.

Walk back down Tai Hang Road and north along Tung Lo Wan Road, turn left into Leighton Road and take the footbridge across to Irving Street and the start of **Jardine's Bazaar**. This was once a popular clothes market, but most of the stalls have moved into the parallel Jardine's Crescent. If it's traditional character you're after, the turtle soup shop, herbalists and pawnbroker's on **Pennington Street** are a better bet.

Turn left along Kai Chiu Road, over Lee Garden Road (home to many 'factory outlet' clothing shops) and the Percival Street tramlines, to **Times Square**, a pristine vertical shopping mall with its own MTR entrance and several highly-rated restaurants, where you can end the tour or break for lunch.

Shopping mall dining is a fashionable facet of the contemporary Hong Kong lifestyle and should definitely be tried at least once. **Bistro Gold** and **Wu Kong** (both on the 12th floor) offer excellent Shanhainese food. If budget's a priority, check out the basement food hall (B2). Whatever you decide, ride the glazed bubble lift up the exterior to the 13th floor to see the dramatic contrast between the ramshackle rooftop gardens of the old Causeway Bay tenements and the high-rises that are fast replacing them.

If you continue after lunch, hop on a tram going south along Percival Street; get a seat upstairs to make the most of the view. As the tram rumbles along Wong Nai Chung Road, notice the elegant classical façade of **St Margaret Mary's Church** perched up the hill on the left and **Happy Valley Racecourse** on your right.

Happy Valley was used for rice cultivation until the 1840s when it was seconded by the British for cemeteries and a rudimentary horse-racing track. Today, the race-course boasts state-of-the-art technology and is surrounded by high-rises, and the atmosphere at the Wednesday evening races during the September–June racing season is electric; Hong Kongers love to gamble – betting figures that run into billions of US dollars each year. The **Hong Kong Racing Museum** (tel: 2966 8065; Tuesday to Sunday and some hol-

idays 10am–5pm; Happy Valley race days 10am–12.30pm) on the second floor of the Happy Valley Stand tells the story in full; and offers a superb view of the racecourse.

The cemeteries (open daily 8am–6pm) on the other side of Wong Nai Chung Road provide further insight into Hong Kong's colonial history and a peaceful respite after the crowds of Causeway Bay. The **Parsi Cemetery** beside the Hindu Temple is the most picturesque with its lush greenery. The older headstones in the **Hong Kong (Colonial) Cemetery** tell of the early settlers' often youthful deaths, while Portuguese memorials in **St Michael's Roman Catholic Cemetery** highlight the link with nearby Macau. There is a surprisingly high number of Chinese names in the **Muslim Cemetery**. The memorials to many prominent Hong Kong citizens in the **Jewish Cemetery** are worth a detour up Shan Kwong Road. When you're ready, you can catch a tram back to Wan Chai or Causeway Bay.

3. Yau Ma Tei and Mong Kok

Experience a more traditional side of Hong Kong culture and pick up some shopping bargains on this walk through the famous markets of Yau Ma Tei and Mong Kok.

Begin from the Bowring Street exit of Jordan MTR station (Exit C2). Walk down Bowring Street, known for its fabric shops and clothes stalls, turn right up Woosung Street, cross busy Jordan Road and head one block west till you come to a shop where they make fresh sugar cane juice and medicinal tonics. Take a right up **Temple Street**, famous for its lively night market (see *Itinerary 11: Kowloon by Dark*). By day, the first couple of blocks are a centre for wholesale jewellery suppliers and you can see traditional jewellers' tools for sale at No 215.

You'll come to a traditional open-fronted tea shop on your left; why not try one of the

Jade Market offerings

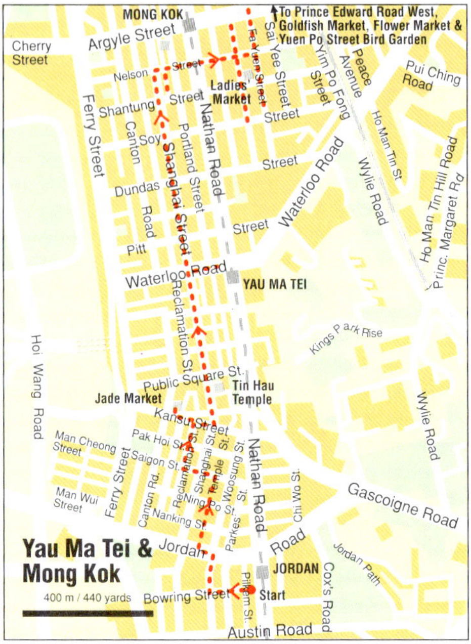

herbal brews if you're thirsty? Turn left here onto **Saigon Street**. The screen inside the doorway of the yellow-tiled Tak Sang pawnshop, on the corner with Shanghai Street, is there for privacy purpose and to prevent evil spirits from entering.

Continue along Saigon Street and turn right up Reclamation Street, with its lively food market (not for the squeamish as this is where many frogs and turtles meet their end), to **Kansu Street**. Beneath the highway bridge is the **Jade Market** (open daily 10am–3.30pm), packed with stalls hawking everything from top-grade jade to cheap glass trinkets. Genuine jade can range in colour from a milky white to a deep translucent green. Fault lines or specks lower the value, and the best stones are uniform in colour and cool to the touch. Jade has many imitations so, unless you're an expert, don't worry about intrinsic worth and stick to pieces which you like for their decorative value. Be prepared to bargain hard and compare prices.

By the small fruit and vegetable market on Kansu Street, take a left turn into **Shanghai Street** and walk north to the 120-year-old (open daily 8am–6pm) Tin Hau Temple. This is really four temples in one. Tin Hau is worshipped in the large temple behind the main entrance, with spirals of incense suspended from the ceiling, an ornate altar with golden effigies and fanciful Chinese lanterns. Fortune-tellers ply their ancient trade at the south end of the complex, and old men play cards and Chinese chess in the park outside.

The next stretch of Shanghai Street is lined with shops selling altar shrines, statues of Buddhist and Taoist deities, and *feng shui* mirrors and compasses. At No 284 is a traditional kitchen implement shop selling bamboo steamers, chopping boards and wooden biscuit-moulds. Further along you will find a small park where elderly men while away the hours with their caged songbirds. The two flag shops on Man Ming Lane opposite are a reminder of the area's former seafaring legacy.

Wooden chopping boards

A blind street-side fortune teller

If your feet are tired, turn right down Waterloo Road to Yau Ma Tei MTR station and ride one stop north to Mongkok station (Nelson Street exit). Otherwise, continue walking north along Shanghai Street as far as Nelson Street. This takes you through the heart of **Yau Ma Tei** ('Place of Sesame Plants'), one of Kowloon's oldest residential and commercial districts.

The area has changed radically with the completion of the massive West Kowloon Reclamation on what was once a bustling typhoon shelter. These days, the old colonnaded buildings have all but disappeared as modern businesses move in and the typhoon shelter has been moved a mile west. However, the connection with the sea is still evident in the seafood restaurants, wet fish trade, traditional metal and leather artisan workshops and a few quaint anachronisms such as On Cheong's shop selling old kerosene ship lamps at No 310 Shanghai Street.

Around the junctions with Soy and Shantung streets, you enter **Mong Kok** ('Busy Place') – one of the densest urban populations in the world and long infamous for bordellos and triad activity. There's been a concerted effort to clean up the vice establishments in recent years and the area is now home to some great open-air markets that are worth visiting.

To reach **Ladies' Market** (open noon–10.30pm), continue east along Nelson Street, under the Nathan Road MTR, to **Tung Choi Street**. Here you'll find hundreds of stalls selling cheap T-shirts, jeans, cheeky lingerie, electronic gadgets and other gimicky souvenirs. Continue north on Tung Choi Street, crossing busy Argyle Street and Mong Kok Road. This end of Tung Choi Street is known as **Goldfish Market** (10am–6pm), where Hong Kong people buy the fish and aquariums considered lucky in *feng shui*. The parallel section of **Fa Yuen Street** is famous for its factory outlet shops and is a good place to pick up genuine fashion bargains.

At the north end of Fa Yuen Street, cross busy Prince Edward Road West, head one block east, take the first left into Sai Yee Street and first right into fragrant Flower Market Road, home to Hong Kong's premier wholesale **Flower Market** (10am–6pm). At the far end you'll find the **Yuen Po Street Bird Garden** (7am–8pm). Here, thousands of songbirds are displayed in intricately fashioned bamboo or wooden cages (which are also for sale at the garden and make great souvenirs). The birds are valued not so much for their appearance but for their singing abilities. Retrace your steps back to Prince Edward Road West and walk east three blocks to Prince Edward MTR station.

Picnic Bay and the waterfront at Sok Kwu Wan

4. Lamma Island

Leave the metropolis behind with this leisurely morning stroll across Lamma Island and a seafood lunch overlooking the bay.

At only 13½sq km (5sq miles), Lamma is the third largest island in the territory after Lantau and Hong Kong Island. Its beautiful topography is somewhat marred by three towering chimney stacks and a coal-fired power station at its northwestern tip, which provides electricity for Hong Kong Island. Still, Lamma's rolling hills, sandy beaches, seafood restaurants and car-free paths make it the ideal getaway from the urban congestion that is Hong Kong.

Some of the Hong Kong city-dwellers who visit Lamma like it so much they stay. The main village, **Yung Shue Wan**, seems to have doubled in size almost overnight as houses shoot up to meet the demand, but the island's population still only hovers around 10,000 and the village has managed to retain much of its Mediterranean-esque charm despite recent development and reclamation works.

This leisurely 90-minute stroll follows a paved path linking the village with Sok Kwu Wan on the east coast. The *Lamma Island Coastal Guide* is a great guide to the island's natural heritage (see *Maps*; also available on Lamma from the Scorpio Business Centre on the right as you head towards Hung Shing Ye beach) and there are map boards posted around the island. To get to Lamma, take a Yung Shue Wan-bound (and not Sok Kwu Wan) ferry from Central Ferry Pier No 5 (10 morning crossings before noon each day). The trip takes 30 minutes on the ordinary ferries and 20 minutes on the fast ferries or catamarans.

Follow **Yung Shue Wan Main Street** from the pier round the harbour past the open-air Chinese restaurants, grocery shops, gift shops and cafés serving Western food. The **Bookworm Café** (open daily 10am–10pm) or traditional *dim sum* at the **Sampan** restaurant are good bets if you haven't had breakfast yet. At the far end, near the sports ground, is a well-tended **Tin Hau** temple, where the goddess' birthday is celebrated each May (see *Calendar of Special Events*).

Lamma island stilted houses

Retrace your steps to the first junction, turn right and follow the path away from the waterfront towards **Hung Shing Ye beach**. The modern tiled-houses gradually peter out and the path winds past small vegetable plots and dotted hamlets, with the ever-present spectre of the power station looming on your right. There is a map board beneath the police station on the right just before you reach Hung Shing Ye beach.

After the beach the path climbs and dips through rural scenery, above rugged cliffs and small sandy bays. A pagoda-style viewing pavilion marks the half-way point of the walk and you can see how far you've come by the map board outside. The path descends into a wooded valley at **Lo So Shing**. Bear right through the sleepy hamlet of traditional Chinese houses and right again at the sign to **Lo So Shing Beach**. Fringed by woodland, this beach is one of the prettiest in Hong Kong, crowded on hot summer weekends but otherwise deserted.

Rejoin the main path and turn right towards **Sok Kwu Wan**. Follow the path along the western rim of **Picnic Bay**, a patchwork of floating fish farms. North side of the bay is scarred by a massive quarry and cement works. The scene looking south towards Mount Stenhouse is unblemished. Look out for the caves on your right where, story has it, Japanese soldiers planned an aborted *kamikaze* attack on the allies at the end of World War II.

Sok Kwu Wan village is famous for seafood and any of the dozen or so restaurants along the waterfront makes an ideal place to stop for lunch. Indeed, relaxing with a cool drink on the stilted terraces overlooking the bay is a favourite escape for Hong Kong residents. Most of them will tell you to choose the busiest and most crowded, but my favourite is the **Wan Kee**, just beyond the well-tended Tin Hau temple as you enter the village, which is worth visiting for its dragon-boat prow adorned with deer antlers. Choose your meal from the fish tanks or ask the waiter for a recommendation (deep fried squid, minced quail and steamed garlic or peppered prawns are popular choices with local expats, who tend to avoid shellfish because of the Hepatitis A-risk factor). There are ferries back to Central every two hours or so (1.10pm, 3pm and 4.45pm on weekdays; 2pm and 4pm on Sunday or holidays), or you can ask the restaurant staff about kaidos and sampans to Aberdeen.

Afternoon Itineraries

5. Wan Chai Afternoon

Explore the back-streets, markets and temples of old Wan Chai and finish up at the gleaming new Hong Kong Convention and Exhibition Centre extension.

This tour starts from Wan Chai MTR exit A3 on O'Brien Road. Head over the Johnston Road tramlines, and proceed down **Tai Yuen Street**. Some of the old buildings are being torn down in the name of 'progress', but this and neighbouring side-streets still retain much of their old Chinese flavour. Look out for the sidewalk printer on **Tai Yuen Street** who will make chops and business cards to order, and the snake shop at No 8A Spring Garden Lane. Walk east through the bustling food markets of Cross Street and Wan Chai Road. Cross Queen's Road East and walk up **Stone Nullah Lane** to the **Pak Tai Temple** (1860s) and take a look at the 3-m (10-ft) copper image of the Taoist god Pak Tai which was made in 1604.

Bustling Wan Chai

Retrace your steps to **Queen's Road East**, which marks Wan Chai's original waterfront and is now known for its rattan and rosewood furniture shops. Head west as far as the former **Wan Chai Post Office** (1912) stands at the corner of Wan Chai Gap Road on the other side of Queen's Road East. The quaint white-washed building served as the territory's oldest post office until 1992. It now houses the **Environmental Resource Centre** (Monday to Saturday 10am–5pm, Wednesday 10am–1pm). Take a look inside at the original wooden counter and red postal boxes; nature lovers can pick up a leaflet on the **Wan Chai Green Trail** which starts at the 80-year-old mango tree and giant candlenut tree just outside.

Head west to the circular **Hopewell Centre**, once the tallest building in town. Ride the glass bubble lift between the 17th and 56th floors for one of the city's most spectacular views. The **Re-**

Wan Chai night: restaurants, nightclubs and neon lights

volving 66 restaurant on the 62nd floor is so-called because it takes 66 minutes to do a complete 360-degree revolution.

Further west is the **Hung Shing (Tai Wong) Temple** (1860). You can smell the incense before you see it. As befits its former waterfront location, the temple is dedicated to one of the patron gods of fishermen. Notice the boulders incorporated into its design and the sacred banyan tree behind.

Cross back over Queen's Road East and walk down **Tai Wong Street East**, a typically eclectic Wan Chai street. At the junction with Johnston Road is the picturesque old **Woo Cheong Pawn Shop**, with distinctive tall counters inside. Turn left one block along Johnston Road and immediately left down Tai Wong Street West and listen to the chirp of songbirds in the small **Wan Chai bird market** before rejoining Queen's Road East. Head west, looking out for the traditional herbalist shop at No 102 and the rice barrels outside No 96, and turn right again into Gresson Street, another crowded and colourful street market. Cross over Johnston Road and walk up **Fenwick Street**. This street takes you past the fringe of Wan Chai's nightlife district (see *Itinerary 10*). Once notorious as a raunchy R&R destination for sailors and servicemen in search of their own Suzie Wong, the girlie bars today compete with trendy bars and restaurants. But in the afternoon, the neon lights are off and all is quiet on the Wan Chai front.

Just before you reach the busy Gloucester Road highway, take the escalator up over the pedestrian bridge. Pause mid-way to

Gresson Street market

The Academy for Performing Arts

look east through the amazing canyon of skyscrapers before re-joining Fenwick Street on the far side. The modern building on your left houses the **Academy for Performing Arts** (APA), a college of dance, music and drama that doubles as a performance venue. Turn right into Harbour Road and you come to the **Hong Kong Arts Centre**, which since 1987, has been another fulcrum of contemporary art and culture. The centre houses exhibition galleries, a theatre, cinema, café and arts bookshop.

Leave the building by the pedestrian bridge beside the bookshop on the second floor and cross over Harbour Road. The first staircase on the right leads down through a small sculpture garden and enter the impressive lobby of the Grand Hyatt. Take the staircase on your right and continue through to the **Hong Kong Convention and Exhibition Centre**. The centre's new extension was completed in 1997, doubling its capacity, and was the venue for the historic Handover Ceremony at midnight on 30 June when China resumed sovereignty. Take the escalator and atrium passage through to the extension. If you're thirsty pause for refreshments and optional Internet browsing at the Cybercafé (open Monday to Friday 7am–6.30pm; to 5.30pm on Sunday). Exit the complex at the northeast end and walk along **Expo Promenade** for dramatic views of Victoria Harbour and Kowloon.

Retrace your steps to the main entrance and follow signs for the **Renaissance Harbour View Shopping Arcade**, where the **TDC Design Gallery** (open Monday to Friday 10am–7pm; Saturday till 6.30pm; closed holidays) promotes 'the best of'

Grand Hyatt lobby

Wan Chai nightclub

Hong Kong design. Continue through the shopping arcade and follow signs for **Central Plaza**, which rises 78 floors to a whopping 374m (1,227ft) and is the tallest building in Hong Kong. Your afternoon in Wan Chai is over. If you're in the mood, go on to explore Wan Chai by night (see *Itinerary 10*). Alternatively, follow the signs back to Wan Chai MTR station or take a Star Ferry over to Tsim Sha Tsui from the nearby Wan Chai Ferry Pier.

6. Hollywood Road

Temples, antiques and backstreets: a district steeped in early colonial history

This tour starts from the western end of Hollywood Road at its junction with Queen's Road West (see map on page 34). A No 5, 5C or 10 bus from the Hongkong Bank building in Central will get you there. As you head up **Hollywood Road** there is a row of shops on the right selling joss sticks, paper offerings for the dead and traditional Chinese coffins.

Across the street, through the Chinese gateway **Hollywood Park** provides the living with a pleasant spot to while away their free time. Old sepia photos displayed on the notice board show how the area looked like a century ago. A little further up Hollywood Road on the left is **Possession Street**, so called because it marks the spot where the British navy landed in 1841 to claim the Hong Kong Island in the name of Queen Victoria. It's hard to imagine now, but

Hollywood Road: antique collector's paradise

Abacus maths

this used to be the waterfront.

Turn right off Hollywood Road into Pound Lane (unsigned, opposite Possession Street). This brings you to **Tai Ping Shan Street**, where Cheung Po Tsai and his legendary pirate band settled after receiving amnesty some 30 years before the British arrived. Notice the tiny earth god shrines on the corners before turning right up to **Paak Sing** or '100 Names' Ancestral Hall, founded in 1856 by early Chinese settlers to house the ancestor tablets they brought with them from China. There are several thousand wooden tablets inside as well as shrines to deities like Kwun Yam, Sui Tsing Paak and Tin Hau.

Follow Tai Ping Shan Street east; the shrine on your left and the vividly-coloured temple further are both dedicated to **Kwun Yam**, the Buddhist Goddess of Mercy. Turn left down Upper Station Street and then right to rejoin Hollywood Road. Art lovers will enjoy browsing in the high-end Chinese antique shops along this stretch. A detour left down stepped Ladder Street takes you past Willow Gallery (a location in the mini-series adaptation of James Clavell's *Taipan*) and left again into Upper Lascar Row, home to the bustling **'Cat Street' flea market**. No one can agree over the origin of this nickname. Some say that cat burglars and pirates used to fence their spoils here; others that street peddlers are known as 'cats' and their wares as 'mouse goods' in Chinese; still others that it's a reference to prostitutes. All are plausible as Upper Lascar Row was once the heart of a crowded Chinese ghetto, notorious for its opium dens, gambling parlours and brothels. What is certain is that people have been trading antiques and second-hand goods here for almost 150 years. Today, the serious dealers operate from shops and most of what you'll see outside in the flea market is junk, but you might still come across the odd 'find'.

Back on Hollywood Road you come to one of the island's

A porcelain figurine at Cat Street

oldest places of worship, **Man Mo Temple** (c.1842), dedicated to the gods of Literature and War; the latter, appropriately enough, is also the guardian of antique dealers.

If you can face any more steps, you can make a detour to the top of Ladder Street to explore the fascinating collection on traditional Chinese and modern Western medicine at the **Museum of Medical Sciences** (Tuesday to Saturday 10am–5pm; Sunday and some holidays 1–5pm). It is housed in the red-brick Old Pathological Institute (1905) on Caine Lane.

Proceeding east along Hollywood Road are dozens of antique and curio stores filled with Oriental furniture, ceramics and *objets d'art.* You can also rummage for Mao memorabilia and old photos of Hong Kong at the open-fronted bric-a-brac shop beneath the escalator near the corner of Lyndhurst Terrace, a road infamous for European prostitutes in Hong Kong's early days as a colony.

Give your feet a rest by riding the **Central-Mid-Levels Escalator** (the world's longest outdoor escalator) a few blocks up Shelley Street to Mosque Street, looking out for the picturesque old Jamia Mosque set in a walled garden off to the left. Wander back down Shelley Street and turn left into Elgin Street, right (briefly) into Peel Street and right again along Staunton Street. This is the heart of SoHo (South of Hollywood Road) home to a score of trendy bars and eateries.

At the end of Staunton Street, turn left into Old Bailey Street. There's a New Age Bookshop on the left and a huge fort-like edifice on your right: the **Central Police Station and Victoria Prison**. This is one of the finest examples of early colonial architecture left and worth a look (visitors are welcome provided they 'report in' first). From here cross Hollywood Road and continue east to Wyndham Street. Many early police constables were ethnic Indians and some of Hong Kong's best oriental carpet shops and Indian restaurants can be found along this stretch. The tour is over now, so why not give one of them a try?

Man Mo Temple

7. Victoria Peak Walk

No trip to Hong Kong would be complete without a ride on the Peak Tram or a walk around the perimeter of Hong Kong's most famous mountain.

Start this itinerary by hopping on the free open-top shuttle bus from the City Hall (east) side of the Star Ferry concourse in Central to the **Peak Tram station** on Garden Road. One of the world's steepest funicular railways, the **Peak Tram** has been running since 1888. Its spectacular 8-minute, 373m (1,223ft) ascent ends at the base of the **Peak Tower** (1997). Designed by British architect Terry Farrell in the shape of an upheld rice bowl, the 7-storey complex boasts some great views from the viewing terrace on Level 5, indoor virtual reality rides and a Ripleys Believe It or Not! Odditorium (open daily 9am–10pm; admission fee).

If the weather is fine, save the indoor attractions for later and make the most of the fresh air. Bearing right past the Peak Tower around into **Lugard Road** is the start of a gentle circular walk around **Victoria Peak**, which takes about one hour to complete. The tree-lined path winds past isolated colonial villas that rank among the most romantic and exclusive homes in the territory. It's a world apart from the bustling high-rise metropolis below. On clear days (which are rare) you can see beyond the busy harbour and Kowloon over to the **Nine Dragon Ridge**, which separates urban Hong Kong from the New Territories. Pause to watch black-eared kites (Hong Kong's commonest bird of prey) float on thermal currents above the city and the hundreds of ships in the harbour.

Lugard Road merges with Harlech Road at a four-path junction and shaded picnic spot. The path winds east along the deeply wooded southern flank of the mountain back to the Peak Tram complex. It's a popular jogging and exercise circuit. Pause for re-

View from Victoria Peak

freshments at the **Peak Café** (1901), an elegant building that was once used as a shelter for sedan chairs and their bearers.

If you're feeling energetic, continue on up steep Mt Austin Road – watching out for fast cars – to **Victoria Peak Gardens**, for more elevated views and greenery. The well-tended gardens are all that remain of the early governors' summer residence. It's a good idea to take mosquito-repellent if you're planning to linger till dusk before wandering back down Mt Austin Road.

Back at the Peak complex, why not pick up a souvenir from one of the many shops in the Peak Galleria (award-winning local designer Alan Chan's shop on Level 2 is a good place to start). Then watch the city light up as darkness settles before taking the tram back to Central. Or else, enjoy the spectacular view with a delicious meal at **Café Deco** (tel: 2849 5111) in the Peak Galleria but book a window table in advance.

8. Cheung Chau Island

Catch a ferry and savour the unique atmosphere of Hong Kong's most densely-populated outer island

Languid day on Cheung Chau

Most of Hong Kong's outer islands are rural, with sparse villages or uninhabited wilderness. But not **Cheung Chau**, where more than 40,000 people are packed into fishing boats and old cinder-block houses on 2½sq km (1sq mile) of land, making it a truly urbanised island. Despite development, the dumbbell-shape island still retains much of its old village atmosphere. To get there, catch a ferry from Central Ferry Pier No 6 (nearly 40 departures a day). Fast ferries take 35–40 minutes, but if you've time buy a ticket for the air-conditioned upper deck of a slow one (50 minutes) and enjoy the view from the back deck upstairs. The ride culminates inside a bustling typhoon shelter.

There's a map of Cheung Chau in the *Hong Kong Guidebook* (see *Maps*) or you can consult the map boards by the ferry pier and at several other points on the island once you arrive. The north end of the island is sparsely vegetated compared with the south end and generally not as scenic, with the exception of the stunning bird's-eye view from the summit of the northern hill.

Cheung Chau bun decorations

From the ferry pier, head left along the **Praya** (harbour promenade). Here there is an abundance of seafood restaurants and sidewalk food stalls, making it a good place to stop for refreshments. Some shops also hire out covered tricycles and bikes by the hour.

You'll come to a sports ground, behind which stands the **Pak Tai Temple** (1783). The statue inside was discovered from the sea in the 1700s. The temple and environs are the focus of the famous **Bun Festival**, when eight days each spring Cheung Chau residents try to dispel 'hungry ghosts'. Tall 18m (60ft) towers of pink and white buns are erected as offerings to the ghosts; a procession winds through the streets with children, richly costumed as figures from Chinese myths or history, who appear to float over the heads of the adults by means of hidden supports.

Turn right out of the temple, past the Home for the Aged archway, and follow the steep, winding path to a modern pagoda and lookout point. Then head back to the harbour and north along industrial Pai Chong Street where an ice factory loads waiting boats by sending the ice along an overhead chute. Wooden junks are still built and repaired at waterfront boat-yards beyond the ice house.

Proceed south of Pak Tai temple down Pak She and San Hing streets – packed with shops and stalls selling joss sticks, food, souvenirs and traditional Chinese herbs – which run along the island's narrow isthmus. Turn left along Tung Wan Road to the beach. Laze the rest of the day away on the sand, hire a windsurfer or kayak, or have a barbecue. The **Cheung Chau Windsurfing Centre and Café** (tel: 2981 8316; open daily 10am–7pm) owned by the uncle of windsurfing champion and 1996 Olympic gold medalist Lee Lai-shan ('San-san') provides lessons as well as rentals. There are do-it-yourself barbecue pits at the southernmost end of **Kwum Yan Wan** (Afternoon Beach; to the right of the Windsurfing Centre as you look at the sea) and you can pick up provisions, charcoal and barbecue forks in the village stores.

For a longer walk, take the Kwun Yam Wan Road path up the hill behind the Warwick Hotel to scenic **Peak Road**. Head south and follow signs down to the rocky coastline at **Nam Tam Wan** (Morning Beach). Continue west along Peak Road and eventually you'll come to a cemetery and then a path down to **Pak Tso Wan** (Italian Beach). Further around the promontory is a **cave** where a notorious Qing dynasty pirate, Cheung Po Tsai, allegedly buried his treasure, and an old Tin Hau temple. Return to the ferry pier for dinner by sampan from Sai Wan village or continue round the coast on the wide road that leads back to the waterfront.

Right, the main Bun Festival procession

中興街新場值理會
飄色
新聞自由

Evening Itineraries

9. Lan Kwai Fong

The favourite stomping ground of yuppie Chinese and expatriate 20 to 30-somethings offers more restaurants and after-dark entertainment per square metre than anywhere else in Hong Kong.

Until the mid-1980s **Lan Kwai Fong** was little more than an obscure Central backstreet of old 'walk-ups'. Its transformation was the brainchild of a few entrepeneurs who realised that the new generation of young overseas-educated Chinese, and expatriate professionals who flocked to Hong Kong during the 1980s, were looking for somewhere more hip to drop their cash than the old dive bars of Wan Chai and Tsim Sha Tsui. Lan Kwai Fong's reputation centred on rowdy boozing and a hipper-than-thou dance scene until a traumatic street-crush in the early minutes of New Year's Day 1993 left 20 youngsters dead and 60 more injured. The period of mourning that followed saw 'the Fong' and its clientele 'grow up'. It is now firmly back on the map as *the* place for having a good time, with designer-chic restaurants outnumbering the bars these days. Such is its success, that it has inspired the creation of a new area of designer bars and restaurants in the streets south of Hollywood Road (**SoHo**).

Oscars at Lan Kwai Fong

The Fong is easy to reach. Every taxi on Hong Kong-side knows the location; or, walk up D'Aguilar Street from Queen's Road Central; there's a signposted exit in Central MTR station. Lan Kwai Fong itself is a short L-shaped lane that intersects D'Aguilar Street at either end. But the action spills over into adjacent streets like D'Aguilar and Wyndham, Wo On Lane and Wing Wah Lane. It's a very compact area and much of the Fong's appeal lies in the fact that you can hop from one bar to another just checking out people and places.

The area comes alive in the evening as yuppie office workers flock to their favourite watering holes. Prime-spots for people-watching include **La Dolce Vita**, a funky Italian bar popular with models and well-heeled

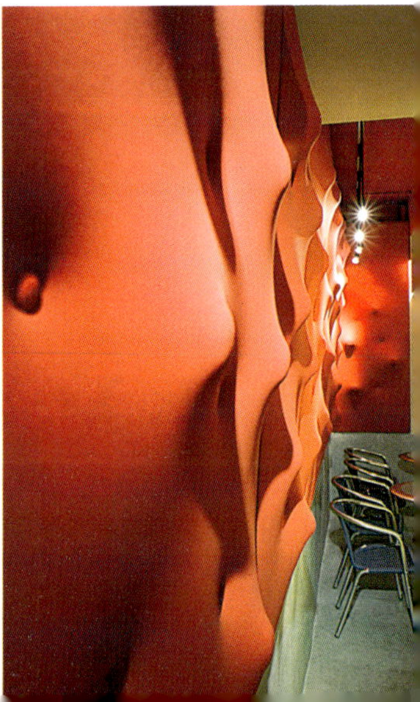
The walls come alive at La Dolce Vita

Al's Diner for funky dining

trendies, and open-fronted **Oscars,** a favourite after-work rendezvous for young executives and designers; while arty young things with more dash than cash tend to hang out at **Club 64** on Wing Wah Lane. For a British pub-atmosphere, try **Mad Dogs** or **Hardy's** on D'Aguilar Street; if schnapps and German beer are your tipples, head for **Schnurrbart's** or **Bit Point**; and for the American bar scene check out **California, Tribeca** or **Sherman's**.

Lan Kwai Fong comes into its own when the hunger pangs come on. There's a medley of world cuisines here and prices range from moderate to off-the-scale; the standard is generally high. Several restaurants rank among Hong Kong's finest and count leading business figures, politicians and celebrities among their clientele. Most are quite small, booking ahead is a good idea.

Reservations are essential for the very classy (and very expensive) **Va Bene** (Italian), **Café des Artistes** (French), **Tutto Meglio** and **Tutta Luna** (Italian). Outstanding Asian restaurants in this league include **China Lan Kwai Fong, Thai Lemongrass, Indochine 1929** (Vietnamese) and the **Wyndham Street Thai** (inspired Aussie-Thai cuisine at decidedly upscale prices). The New Age sushi at **Tokio Joe** is slightly more affordable.

The al fresco balcony at **American Pie** or the **Papillon** French bistro at Wo On Lane are good spots for low-key romantic dinners. Late-nighters, vegetarians and the indecisive will love **Post 97** where the menu's as eclectic as the clientele. For a more traditional and down-to-earth locale, try **Il Mercato**, a convival Italian trattoria; **Yorohachi**, a cosy Japanese with good-value sets; American **Al's Diner** and **Trio's,** a friendly seafood and steak bistro down Wo On Lane; or pub-grub in **Mad Dogs**. There's also the cheap, no-frills **Good Luck Thai** café on Wing Wah Lane, several fast-food outlets, and take-out falafels and kebabs at **Midnight Express**.

After dinner, jazz aficionados should make a bee-line for **The Jazz and Blues Club**. There are regular 'unplugged' sessions at **Hardy's Folk Club** and it's worth checking if anyone's performing at the nearby **Fringe Club**. Newer live music venues include **Insomnia** and **Gig**.

Dance options depend on whether you can enter the trendy but private **Club 97**; get near the tiny dance floor in **California.** But fear not, the lively street-scene outside can be just as much fun; bars stay open to the early hours of the morning.

Working off work stress

Wan Chai welcome

10. Wan Chai by Night

Dance clubs, live music pubs, performing arts, cinema and top-notch hotel entertainment vie with the sleazy girlie-bars of Suzie Wong fame. Mix your own Wan Chai cocktail and join the best party in town.

Wan Chai shot to fame with Richard Mason's 1957 best-seller *The World of Suzie Wong* and the popular 1960 film version starring William Holden and Nancy Kwan. Sleazy girlie-bars, glitzy hostess joints and neon still line the streets of Wan Chai's core nightlife district and on Friday and Saturday nights, there's a decidedly rakish, cruisey buzz in the air. But late-1990s Wan Chai offers a far more eclectic mix of night-time entertainment than it did during its heyday as a raunchy R&R retreat for US servicemen during the Korean and Vietnam wars.

If you're a fan of contemporary arts or a film-buff, start by checking out what's on at the Academy for Performing Arts, HK Arts Centre or **Cine-Art House** in the Sun Hung Kai Centre. For a relaxing, low-key evening, you could combine a show with a quiet meal in one of the numerous restaurants in the area, but, the outing could just as easily lead on to a lively night on the town as Wan Chai's bars and discos stay open till dawn.

There are restaurants for every budget. **Grissini's** and **One Harbour Road** in the Grand Hyatt combine top-notch Italian and Cantonese fare with sensational harbour views and upscale glamour. Reservations and full wallets are essential for the gourmet Cantonese restaurant **Fook Lam Moon**, at No 35–45 Johnston Road.

But you don't have to spend a mint to eat well here, particularly if you enjoy Asian food. Tasty Thai fare is found at **Phukets**, No 44 Hennessy Road, **Chili Club** and **Lotus Thai** at No 88 and No 93–107 Lockhart Road. If you're in a creative mood, try the all-you-can-eat fresh Mongolian barbecue at **Kublai's**, No 18 Luard Road, where you select your own ingredients and sauces for the chef to cook. There's cheap Vietnamese food at **Saigon Beach**, No 66 Lockhart Road; Malaysian curries at **Coconut Curry House** in Kwan Chart Tower, 6 Tonnochy Road; and Filipino, Indonesian and Malaysian cuisines plus a lively party atmosphere at **Cinta,** 10 Fenwick Street. The **Sun Hung Kai Centre** offers three highly-rated choices: Indian and southeast Asian fare at **The Viceroy**; modern Italian at **Milano** and contemporary Vietnamese at **Saigon**. The Viceroy (tel: 2827 7777) holds salsa nights every Wednesday.

Despite its name, the ever-popular **American** at No 20 Lockhart Road has been serving inexpensive Peking food for 50 years; **Steam & Stew Inn** at No 21–23 Tai Wong Street East offers tasty MSG-free Chinese fare; or, for fast-food with a difference, try out some of the traditional hawker soups and noodle dishes at the (govern-

ment-approved) **Hawker Noodle** at No 146 Queen's Road East. For something more familiar, head east to **Harry Ramsden's** at No 213 for traditional fisn 'n chips and mushy peas (note that the chips are cooked in lard).

Drinking spots are just as varied; ranging from the Grand Hyatt's very classy **Champagne Bar** down to seedy dives and girlie-bars on Lockhart, Luard and Jaffe roads and Fenwick Street, with a selection of popular pubs and bars in between.

If you enjoy live music, head to **The Wanch**, a well-established, down-to-earth pub at No 54 Jaffe Road or **Delaney's**, a smart, lively Irish pub at No 18 Luard Road. Newer live music venues include **Johnny B Goode** at No 81–85 Lockhart Road (happy hour till 10pm); and **Dusk Till Dawn** at No 76 Jaffe Road. **Rick's Café** at No 78 Jaffe Road is a bar with a dance floor that stays open late and gets packed with a fun crowd while **Time After Time** has a clubby feel at No 118. **Carnegie's,** at No 53–55 Lockhart Road, is a relatively up-scale American-style bar with good music and a party atmosphere, popular with the 30-something crowd; **The Flying Pig** pub at No 81–85 attracts a lively young crowd determined to party; while the delightfully seedy **Old China Hand** at No 104 is a favourite with the older expatriate crowd.

Delaney's for Irish beers

If it's top-of-the-line ambience you're after, the capacious and glitzy **JJ's** in the Grand Hyatt has been voted the best nightclub in town since 1989 and attracts a jet-setting crowd who come to let off steam to disco-music or upbeat transatlantic sounds from the resident American band upstairs.

The smaller but equally upscale and trendy **Manhattan Westworld** in the **Renaissance Harbour View** has a more Chinese flavour with karaoke as well as funky house sounds from around the globe (Ladies night on Thursday), while **Kara Karaoke** on Level 3 of the adjoining Convention Plaza is *the* place for seasoned karaoke aficionados. **Joe Banana's** nightclub at No 23 Luard Road is popular with sporty types and the 30-something plus crowd.

For a raunchier atmosphere and seriously good dance music, check out **The Big Apple** at No 20 Luard Road and **Neptune Disco II** at No 98–108 Jaffe Road. There's a bit of a girlie-bar scene at the latter and neither would win any awards for stylish decor or sophistication, but the resident DJs play some of the hottest, most eclectic dance music in town.

Club BBoss: an extravagant Japanese-style hostess bar

11. Kowloon by Dark

From street market opera to Celtic rock pubs, from dancing to reggae in a Caribbean café to the big band sounds of a 1930s-style Shanghai nightclub, from 'dai pai dong' to posh dining, Kowloon is one big neon playground where anything goes.

Wander through **Temple Street Night Market** (best 7–10pm) which runs from three blocks west of Jordan MTR station (exit A) north to Man Ming Lane by Yau Ma Tei MTR. Although popular with tourists, this is where the locals come to bargain for cheap clothes, leather goods, CDs and electronic gadgetry. But there's more than just shopping: you can consult the palm-readers and fortune-tellers who set up their tables near the Tin Hau Temple; catch impromptu performances of traditional Cantonese opera; and feast on fresh seafood or sweet and savoury snacks known as *siu yei* from inexpensive *dai pai dong* food-stalls on the sidewalk.

If you prefer eating indoors, there's a wonderful old-style **Peking Restaurant** (no credit cards) upstairs at 227 Nathan Road. Alternatively, take the MTR back to Tsim Sha Tsui where you'll find all types of cuisines and an equally varied choice of nightspots.

For the ultimate in fine dining, head to one of the restaurants in The Peninsula hotel. **Gaddi's**, the epitome of classic French elegance, requires a reservation and a very full wallet; as does the **Spring Moon**, which serves exquisite Cantonese dishes in a Chinese art deco setting. For a more affordable taste of luxury try the **Lobby** where the air is filled with rich chatter and the sounds of the resident orchestra. Designer buffs should make a bee-line for **Felix**, Philippe Starck's stunning, avant garde 'brasserie for the 21st century' at the top of The Peninsula; or, re-capture the glamour of nightlife in 1930s Shanghai at the Regent's **Club Shanghai**. Another fun hotel nightspot is the Sheraton's **Someplace Else**.

Moving up Nathan Road, the superb Shanghainese restaurant **Wu Kong** is found in the basement of No 27–33; very cheap but cheerful Indian restaurants tucked away in Chungking Mansions – **Delhi Club Mess** and **Khyber Pass**; and there's some of the classiest modern European food in town at the **Avenue** in the Holiday Inn Golden Mile. If budget's a priority, try one of the best.

Heading east along Humphrey's Avenue, there's a traditional French bistro **Au Trou Normand** at No 6 Carnarvon Road and a lively British pub **Oxford Circus** at No 3–7A Prat Avenue. For something Chinese, **Jade Garden** on the corner of Carnarvon Road and Hart Avenue serves classic Cantonese and **Great Shanghai** at No 26 Prat Avenue offers Shanghainese home-style cooking.

To escape the hustle and bustle of Tsim Sha Tsui, head north to Knutsford Terrace and enjoy a relaxed evening at the designer-chic Italian **Tutto Bene** restaurant or with live Spanish music at either **El Cid Spanish Restaurant** or the **El Cid Tapas & Wine Bar**. There's more live music at **Chasers** pub; while the mellow sounds and Caribbean beach party atmosphere at **Bahama Mama's** are sure to get you dancing. There's more late-night dance action at **Rick's Café** on the parallel Kimberley Road (at No 53–59).

West of Nathan Road, you'll find the popular **Kangaroo Pub** on Haiphong Road; tasty introductions to Indonesian and Taiwanese cuisines at the tiny **Java Rijsttafel** and **Grand Hill** (open till 4am) on Hankow Road. **Ned Kelly's Last Stand**, on Ashley Road, offers pub-grub and exuberant live music; and it'd be hard to fault either food or service at **Jimmy's Kitchen** or **Gaylord Indian**, two of the city's oldest dining establishments. **Delaney's** pub on Peking Road offers Irish fare and traditional Irish music alternating with unplugged Celtic rock.

At the intersection of Hankow and Peking roads, you'll find **Bottoms Up**, a topless dive featured in the 007-movie *The Man With The Golden Gun*, lingering together with **Red Lips** as rather tame survivors of the once notoriously sleazy nightlife district. The main hostess scene takes place in huge, glitzy and mega-expensive Japanese-style nightclubs like **Club BBoss** over in Tsim Sha Tsui East.

Canton Road offers diversions for all the family: North of Haiphong Road you'll find the very clean, cheap and cheerful **Happy Garden Noodle and Congee Kitchen**; a tasty assortment of sweet and savoury dishes at **Sweet Dynasty**; and Kowloon's **Hard Rock Café** is a must for rock and roll fans. Further south, you can dine at **Planet Hollywood**; or at **Peking Garden** in Star House; or at **Dan Ryan's Chicago Grill** in Ocean Terminal.

Excursions

12. Lantau Island

Take a ferry over to Hong Kong's largest island to see the Big Buddha, Po Lin Monastery, Tai O village and Tung Chung Fort.

Majestic and ruggedly mountainous, **Lantau** is more than twice the size of Hong Kong Island – yet still largely rural in character. Lantau's country parks, beaches and coastal villages make it a popular retreat for Hong Kong residents who come here to hike, camp or barbecue on weekends and holidays. But the peace and seclusion of Lantau, which was ideal for monasteries, is slowly being eroded. Up until the early 1960s, when the South Lantau Road was constructed, much of the island was only accessible by boat or foot.

Today, Hong Kong's international airport stands at **Chek Lap Kok** on the north-western coast, and there are plans for a major port development on the north. But, for the moment, Lantau still retains much of its captivating lost-in-the-clouds aura.

The main sights can be covered in a day but start early and try to avoid Sundays and public holidays when the ferries are packed.

Entrance to Po Lin, the 'precious lotus' monastery

A Buddhist nun sweeps the main courtyard at Po Lin

Catch the 8.30am air-conditioned triple-decker ferry or 9am fast ferry to **Mui Wo (Silvermine Bay)** from Central Ferry Pier No 7 (Monday to Saturday; on Sunday and holidays the 8.30am is a fast ferry and the 9am a triple-decker).

At Mui Wo, take a No 2 bus to **Ngong Ping** for Po Lin Monastery (35 minutes past the hour; more frequent on Sundays and holidays). The 40-minute ride takes you past lovely coastal scenery, including beautiful **Cheung Sha**, Hong Kong's longest beach, and into the mountains.

Po Lin Monastery is the largest of Hong Kong's Buddhist temples, a sprawling complex of temples, gateways, gardens and the world's largest seated outdoor **bronze Buddha**, a massive 202-ton figure that looks serenely down on the community and surrounding tea fields. While many tourists come here, it is also a major point of pilgrimage for Hong Kong's Buddhists, who come to pay their respects and pray. Climbing the 268 steps to the base of the statue grants a great view over the surrounding countryside. Since its consecration in 1993, Po Lin is no longer the quiet retreat it once was except for very early in the morning before the hawkers and coach tours arrive. Po Lin was founded by three humble monks in 1905 who wanted a quiet retreat away from the hustle and bustle of Hong Kong. The complex was small and insignificant until 1970 when the main temple and its surrounding structures were opened. Dominating the main hall are three Golden Buddhas; the one in the middle is Sakyamuni, founder of the faith.

You can eat a Chinese vegetarian lunch in the monastery or pick up a snack from one of the stalls that have sprung up outside. But it might be more fun to bring a picnic and find a quiet spot. If you feel energetic, follow the path past the Tea Gardens and take the steep trail to the top of **Lantau Peak** (934m/3,064ft) Hong Kong's

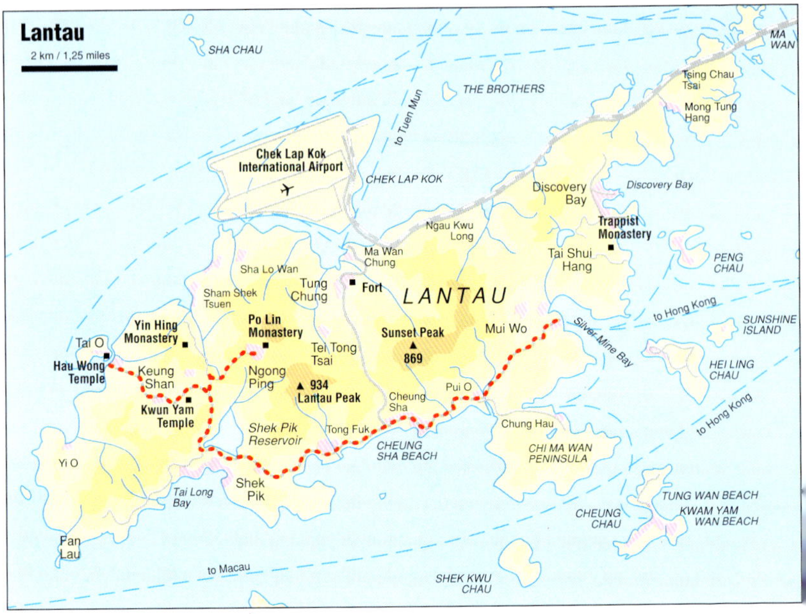

second tallest mountain popular spot for glorious panoramic views.

After lunch take bus No 21 to Tai O (15 minutes past the hour 11.15am–3.15pm). The 20-minute journey passes several splendid monasteries hidden in the hills. **Tai O** is a fascinating old fishing village built on stilts, although its character is changing as modern apartment blocks replace the metal-sheeted wooden structures. The village was originally famed for its salt production and old salt pans can still be seen. Over-fishing has led to a decline in the fishing industry but dried fish, a speciality of Tai O, is still found.

It's worth walking past the old stilt houses to **Hau Wong Temple** (1699). Built on a narrow spit of land surrounded by water, this is the oldest of four temples in the territory dedicated to the guardian of the Song dynasty boy emperors during their period of exile in Hong Kong. As befits a village of fisherfolk, huge whale bones and swordfish beaks are stacked inside.

From Tai O, take a No 11 bus to **Tung Chung Town Centre** (15 and 45 minutes past the hour; the journey takes 50 minutes). From here you can head straight back to Kowloon and Hong Kong Island by MTR (30 minutes). Or, linger a while to visit the early 19th-century Chinese **Tung Chung Fort** and savour the almost surreal juxtaposition of **Tung Chung 'old town'**, with its traditional stilt houses and picturesque Hau Wong Temple, against the backdrop of **Chep Lap Kok International Airport**.

Tai O fish market

13. New Territories

A circular tour offering an insight into the ancient and modern faces of Hong Kong's largest land mass.

The New Territories offer such a diversity of landscapes and sights that it's impossible to make a comprehensive tour of the region in a day. This itinerary, which already packs a very full day by concentrating on the highlights, entails travel by public transportation. Not all of the scenery en route is picturesque, but this is as authentic a part of the Hong Kong experience as the well-trodden sights of Kowloon and Hong Kong Island. Pick and choose the places which sound most appealing, and start the day early. Take plenty of small change for the buses and LRT. A bilingual map such as the *Hong Kong Guidebook* (see *Maps*) would also be helpful as several of the sights are only signposted in Chinese.

Start your day by taking the MTR to Tsuen Wan station (Exit B). From here you have a choice of activities. If you're interested in airports or engineering feats, take a No 96M maxicab to Ting Kau to see the **Airport Core Programme Exhibition Centre** (Tuesday to Friday 10am–5pm; weekends and some holidays 10am–6.30pm). Besides airport-related exhibits, the centre offers good views of the 2.2km-long **Tsing Ma Bridge**, the world's longest road-and-rail suspension bridge.

Otherwise, follow the signs from Exit B to the **Sam Tung Uk Museum** (Wednesday to Monday 9am–5pm) on Kwu Uk Lane. Housed in a Hakka walled village founded by the Chan clan in 1786, this gem of a museum displays period Hakka furniture and farming implements, and exhibitions on Chinese folk culture. The architecture is a striking contrast to the modern housing estates

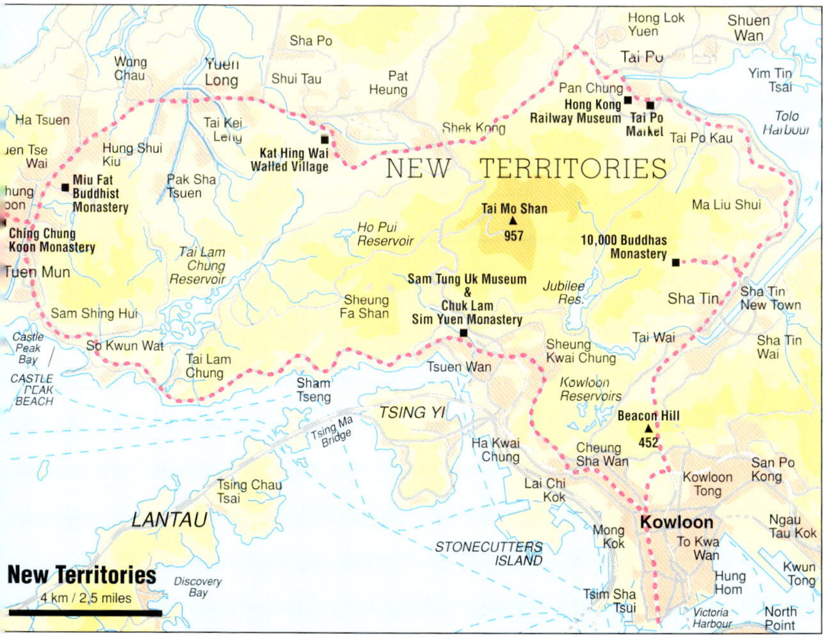

Ancestor worship hall at Ching Chung Koon Monastery

that surround it. You can continue walking (20 minutes uphill) to **Chuk Lam Sim Yuen Monastery**, but as the path isn't signposted, it's easy to get lost. Or, take a No 85 maxicab from Shui Wo Street, just south of the MTR station, and get off at the last stop. The monastery has a Thai-style shrine outside. The main hall houses three golden Buddhas.

Take the No 85 maxicab back to Shiu Wo Street, cross Castle Peak Road by the pedestrian bridge and follow the overhead walkways back to the MTR station. Follow the MTR Exit A2 signs to the bus terminus beneath the CRC Department Store and board a No 66M double-decker bus to the Tai Hing housing estate in Tuen Mun. The front seat on the top deck offers views of the coast and the Tsing Ma Bridge as the bus winds along Tuen Mun Road. The journey takes 30–40 minutes. Get off the bus at its Tai Hing Estate terminus, turn right out of the terminus along Tai Fong Street and left onto the Tsun Wen Road. You can see the roof of your next destination, the Taoist **Ching Chung Koon Monastery** ahead, just beyond the highway bridge. The monastery is dedicated to one of the Eight Immortals and contains picturesque pavilions, lotus ponds and bonsai trees.

Leave the monastery by the path to the left of the one you entered by. You'll see the Ching Chung Light Rail Transit (LRT) stop ahead. Cross the tracks and take the No 615 for 11 stops to the **Fung Nin Road** stop in Yuen Long. Keep an eye out for the **Miu Fat Buddhist Monastery** across

The Main Worship Hall

the main highway, with a flamboyant pair of golden dragons crawling up its three-storey façade.

The Fung Nin Road stop exits onto Castle Peak Road. Follow the railway line east to the Yuen Long West bus station on Kik Yueng Road. If you're hungry, pick up a snack at the bus station. Then catch a No 64K bus marked Tai Po KCR.

If you're racing to get to Tai Po (40 minutes away) stay on the bus; otherwise, get off opposite the Mung Yeung Public School in **Kam Tin Shi** (about 15 minutes). Continue east on foot and follow the signs to **Kat Hing Wai Village**, just south of Kam Tin Road on the right. Kat Hing Wai is the most easily accessible of the group of Hakka walled villages that trace their roots back to the 10th century when the Tang clan moved to this valley from southern China. The buildings inside have been modernised but the way of life is still fairly traditional so it's worth paying the HK$1 donation to enter. If you want to take a photograph of the pipe-smoking Hakka women in their fringed hats, negotiate a small fee beforehand.

Return to the Kam Tin Shi bus stop and get back on No 64K. The bus winds south past Shek Kong and on through the lush **Lam Tsuen Valley**, with lofty **Tai Mo Shan**, Hong Kong's tallest mountain at 957m (3,139ft) off to the south. Keep an eye out for a huge ribboned banyan tree on your left. Villagers have venerated the banyan trees near the little temple at **Lam Tsuen** for centuries and these days people come from all over Hong Kong to ask the **Wishing Tree** for divine assistance.

Aim to get here by 4pm if you want to visit the **Hong Kong Railway Museum** (Wednesday to Monday 9am–5pm) at 13 Shung Tak Street off On Fu Road. If you have a map, you could get off the No 64K bus at the first stop south of Lam Tsuen River. Otherwise, it's best to take a taxi from the KCR station (you'll probably need to show the driver the Chinese name of the museum). The museum is housed in the original **Tai Po Market Railway Station** (1913), a picturesque structure which looks more like a Chinese temple than a train station. Round off your visit with a wander round the traditional market and **Man Mo Temple** on Fu Shin Street near the museum. Next take a Kowloon-bound train from the Tai Po Market KCR station. If you get on the train by 4.15pm, it is worth stopping at Sha Tin station to visit the **Man Fat Tze** or **Monastery of Ten Thousand Buddhas** (9am–5pm).

End the trip by taking the Kowloon-bound KCR south to Kowloon Tong station where you can transfer to the MTR for the onward journey to Tsim Sha Tsui or Hong Kong Island.

Monastery of 10,000 Buddhas

14. MacLehose Trail & Wong Tai Sin Temple

An exhilarating ridge-walk and a visit to Wong Tai Sin Temple.

The first leg of this tour takes in the **Lion Rock Country Park** segment of the **MacLehose Trail**, a rugged 100-km (62-mile) hiking path that stretches from Sai Kung peninsula to Tuen Mun, through some of the wildest countryside in Hong Kong. Allow four hours for this 10-km (6-mile) long segment as it involves a few strenuous climbs. Wear good walking shoes, take along plenty of water, food, rain gear (as clouds can descend suddenly on the peaks) and sun-protection during summer months. Don't underestimate these precautions, especially if you're not used to the climate. Although the trail is signposted, it's a good idea to pick up a MacLehose Trail map from the Government Publications Centre (see *Maps*). For the less intrepid, the Wong Tai Sin Temple leg is rewarding on its own and easily reached by MTR.

Wong Tai Sin Temple

To reach the start of the hike, take a No 81 bus from Nathan Road, two blocks north of Jordan MTR (Exit A), immediately after the Ning Po Street junction. Alight at the **Eagle's Nest (Tsim Shan) Nature Trail** and take the footbridge to the other side of the road. Find the MacLehose Trail sign (symbol is a person with a rucksack and distance markers) and follow the Eagle's Nest Nature Trail to marker No 15, where there is a MacLehose Trail map. Follow Stage 5 of the MacLehose Trail behind the summit of **Eagle's Nest** at 312m (1,023ft). From here you can see the next landmark: 457-m (1,499ft) **Beacon Hill**, with a white-domed radar station at the top. There are stunning views as the trail leads down Beacon Hill, around the back of **Lion Rock** (495m/1,633ft), along the top of **Unicorn Ridge** and down to **Sha Tin Pass**. There's a foodstall with cold drinks just up the road on the left after you exit the arched entrance to Lion Rock Park. Return to the flatlands by way of the wooded path through **Kwun Yam Temple** and on to the bus station beside the **Tsz Oi housing estate** below.

From here you can take a No 3C bus all the way to China HK City in Tsim Sha Tsui. Or, get off at Wong Tai Sin MTR station and follow the signs to the **Wong Tai Sin Temple** (open daily 7am–5.30pm; small donation expected), one of Hong Kong's largest and busiest temples.

Eating Out

Eating is quintessential to the Hong Kong experience. In fact, it's been said that Hong Kong people don't eat to live, they live to eat. A browse through town during mealtime confirms this: almost every place is packed, from lowly *dai pai dong* street stalls to posh restaurants and private dining clubs.

Cantonese cuisine is indigenous to Hong Kong and southern China. The accent is on subtle flavours and the freshest of ingredients. Many Cantonese dishes are now famous around the globe: sweet and sour pork, shark's fin soup and spring rolls. But there are literally thousands of dishes made from a wide variety of ingredients as diverse as bird's nest, sea cucumber and bamboo shoot. And thanks to the millions of mainland Chinese who've resettled in Hong Kong, there are restaurants serving Shanghainese, Beijing, Sichuan, Chiu Chow, Hakka and Taiwanese food. There are many overlapping influences, but when taken as a whole these cuisines are as different as, say, Italian and French. One culinary experience every visitor to Hong Kong should try at least once is the tradition of *yum cha* (drinking tea) with *dim sum* (small snacks; literally, little hearts) for a leisurely breakfast or light lunch.

Hong Kong's increasingly cosmopolitan flavour is reflected in the diverse range of restaurants that have opened in the last decade: Thai, Indonesian, Filipino, Japanese, Korean, Nepali, Vietnamese and Burmese (Indian food has a longer history in Hong Kong as

Jumbo is one of several floating eateries in Aberdeen Harbour

there has been an Indian community here since mid-19th century). Add to this is an increasing number of Western eateries, and it's no exaggeration to say that Hong Kong now offers more choice than just about any city on the planet. Prices quoted below are based on the average cost of a three-course meal (or the Asian equivalent) for two without beverages: \$ = below HK\$300; \$\$ = HK\$300–500; \$\$\$ = above HK\$500–800; \$\$\$\$ = over HK\$800.

Chinese

CARRIANNA CHIU CHOW
151 Gloucester Road, Wan Chai
Tel: 2511 1282 and
Hilton Tower, Tsim Sha Tsui East
Tel: 2724 4828
Some of the best value Chiu Chow food in town, except luxury items like shark's fin. Go for staples like fried e-fu noodles and pomfret fish. \$\$–\$\$\$

DIM SUM
63 Sing Woo Road, Happy Valley
Tel: 2834 8893
Wonderful *dim sum* in a retro-nostalgia setting. \$–\$\$

GREAT SHANGHAI
26 Prat Avenue, Tsim Sha Tsui
Tel: 2366 8158
This massive eatery with a 400-item menu lives up to its name. Tasty traditional home-style cooking from Shanghai and the Yangtze River region. \$–\$\$

HAN LOK YUEN RESTAURANT
16–17 Hung Shing Ye
Yung Shue Wan, Lamma Island
Tel: 2982 0680
Relaxed family-run restaurant with a terrace overlooking Hung Shing Ye beach. Minced quail in lettuce and roast pigeon are the house specialities but seafood dishes are also good. Closed Monday. \$

JUMBO FLOATING RESTAURANT
Shum Wan, Wong Chuk Hang
Aberdeen Harbour
Tel: 2553 9111
A theatrically-decorated palace of twinkling lights in the middle of a junk and yacht-choked waterway. The food's only so-so but the unabashedly kitschy setting is memorable. \$–\$\$

KUNG TAK LAM SHANGHAI VEGETARIAN RESTAURANT
31 Yee Wo Street, Causeway Bay
Tel: 2890 3127 and
1st Floor, 45 Carnarvon Road
Tel: 2367 7881
Imaginative and, if requested, MSG-free vegetarian fare from a renowned family enterprise established in Shanghai since the 1800s. \$–\$\$

LUK YU TEA HOUSE
24–26 Stanley Street, Central
Tel: 2523 5463
A 1930s tea house with an atmosphere that is classic: dark wooden booths, marble-backed chairs, brass spittoons and surly waiters. Some of the best *dim sum* in town. \$\$

MAN WAH
25th Floor, Mandarin Oriental Hotel
5 Connaught Road, Central

Tel: 2522 0111
Gracious service combined with stunning harbour views and elegant surroundings make this one hard to beat. Mouthwatering Cantonese food complemented by Imperial dishes and a superb wine list. Smart dress and reservation essential. $$$$

ONE HARBOUR ROAD
8th Floor, Grand Hyatt Hotel
1 Harbour Road, Wan Chai
Tel: 2588 1234
The classic Cantonese menu, wine list and service are all top-notch. The setting is stunning, complete with trees and lily pond and spectacular harbour views. Smart dress and reservation essential. $$$–$$$$

PEKING GARDEN
Alexandra House, 6 Ice House Street
Central (and other locations)
Tel: 2526 6456
An enjoyable introduction to northern Chinese cuisine, including the famous Peking duck; order beggar's chicken and get to join in the clay-breaking ceremony. $$–$$$

PEKING RESTAURANT
1st Floor, 227 Nathan Road, Jordan
Tel: 2730 1315
Unpretentious old-style restaurant serving delicious, authentic Peking food. The Peking duck is a must. (no credit cards.) $

RED PEPPER
7 Lan Fong Road, Causeway Bay
Tel: 2577 3811
Spicy Szechuan food is a perennial favourite with expats and tourists but service can be a bit brusque. $$–$$$

STEAM & STEW INN
21–23 Tai Wong Street East, Wan Chai
Tel: 2529 3913
Tasty casseroles and other homely, MSG-free Cantonese and Shanghainese fare served with unusual nutty red rice. Frequented by local political luminaries and often packed. Reservation essential. $–$$

TIN TIN SEAFOOD HARBOUR
4th Floor, Elizabeth House
250 Gloucester Road, Causeway Bay
Tel: 2833 6683 (and other locations)
Boisterous Cantonese seafood palace where staff communicate by walkie-talkie. Choose from a selection of fish and crustaceans in tanks. $$

YUNG KEE
32–40 Wellington Street, Central
Tel: 2522 1624
A local dining institution for over 50 years, this Cantonese restaurant is famous for its speciality roast goose. Its four floors can accommodate as many as 1,000 diners at one sitting. $$

Other Asian

BANANA LEAF CURRY HOUSE
440 Jaffe Road, Wanchai
Tel: 2573 8187 (and other locations)
Popular Malaysian restaurant serving a delectable medley of Malay, Indian and Straits Chinese favourites on banana leaves instead of plates. $–$$

GAYLORD
1st Floor, Ashley Centre
23–25 Ashley Road, Tsim Sha Tsui
Tel: 2376 1001/1991
One of the oldest and plushest Indian restaurants in town. $$

GO GU JANG KOREAN BARBECUE
3rd Floor, Caroline Centre
28 Yun Ping Road, Causeway Bay
Tel: 2577 2021
Nibble on spring onion pancakes while watching marinated meat and fish sizzle on a table-top hotplate. $$

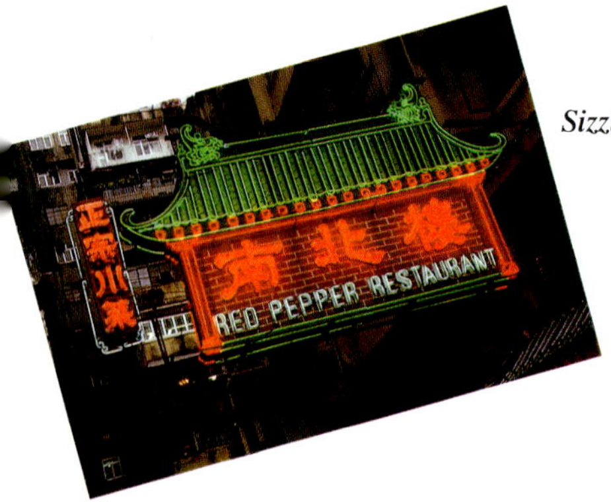

Sizzling Szechuan cuisine

HER THAI
Tower 1, China Hong Kong City Canton Road, Tsim Sha Tsui
Tel: 2735 8898
Excellent Thai food with the added attraction of panoramic views. $$

INDOCHINE 1929
California Tower, 30–32 D'Aguilar Street, Lan Kwai Fong, Central
Tel: 2869 7399
Designer-chic recreation of yesteryear Vietnam. Excellent food and the verandah-style interior evokes images of bygone French colonial elegance. $$$

KOH-I-NOOR
1st Floor California Entertainment Building, 34 D'Aguilar Street, Central
Tel: 2877 9706 (and other locations)
Delicately spiced Mughlai, tandoori and other delicious fare from northern India. $–$$

KUBLAI'S
3rd Floor, One Capital Place
18 Luard Road, Wan Chai
Tel: 2529 9117 (and other locations)
All-you-can-eat Mongolian barbecue restaurant. Excellent food and good value for money. $

NADAMAN
7th Floor Island Shangri-La Hotel, Pacific Place, 88 Queensway, Admiralty
Tel: 2820 8570
Gracious service and elegant surroundings heighten the gastronomic pleasure of fine Japanese cuisine. $$$$

RANGOON
Hoi Kung Building, 265 Gloucester Road, Causeway Bay
Tel: 2893 2281/2893 0778
Warm, friendly little place offering a rare chance to sample Burmese food outside of Myanmar. $

TOKIO JOE
16 Lan Kwai Fong, Central
Tel: 2525 1889
Pleasantly *avant garde* sushi bar and Japanese restaurant with good value set lunches. $$$

WOODLANDS INTERNATIONAL
Ground Floor, Mirador Tower
61 Mody Road, Tsim Sha Tsui East
Tel: 2369 3718
Good Indian vegetarian food in a relaxed environment. Try the crispy *dosai* pancakes and *thali* appetisers. $

East-West

CAFE DECO BAR & GRILL
Level 1 & 2, Peak Galleria
118 Peak Road, The Peak
Tel: 2849 5111
Eclectic menu strong on pizza, tandoori and Thai. Spectacular city views and live jazz each evening. Dinner reservations advised, especially for one of the window tables. $$–$$$

JIMMY'S KITCHEN
Basement, 1–3 Wyndham Street, Central
Tel: 2526 5293 and
1st Floor, 29 Ashley Road, Tsim Sha Tsui
Tel: 2376 0327
Around since 1928, with an eclectic menu featuring traditional favourites of Chinese, Western and Asian kitchens. Consistently good value. $$

LA RONDA
30th Floor, Hotel Furama Hong Kong,

Central
Tel: 2848 7422
Sumptuous international buffet spread (12.30–2.30pm and 6.30–10.30pm) and stunning views as the restaurant revolves through 360 degrees every hour and 15 minutes. Lunch is kinder on the wallet than dinner. $$–$$$

PEAK CAFE
121 Peak Road, The Peak
Tel: 2849 7868
Good Mediterranean and pan-Asian fare in a picturesque old colonial building. The leafy terrace is perfect for romantic dinners. High on charm and very popular so book ahead. $$–$$$

WYNDHAM STREET THAI
38 Wyndham Street, Central
Tel: 2869 2616
Inspired Thai food with an Australian slant in a designer-chic minimalist setting. Good wine list. Reservations advised. $$$–$$$$

Western

AMERICAN PIE
4th Floor California Entertainment Building, 34–36 D'Aguilar Street, Central
Tel: 2877 9779
New England eatery famous for its sublime desserts. The Mississippi mud and banana cream pies, and New York cheesecake are positively sinful. $$

CASA LISBOA
21 Elgin Street, SoHo, Central
Tel: 2869 9631
Traditional Portuguese fare, enthusiastic young staff and a warm, southern European ambience. $$

DAN RYAN'S CHICAGO GRILL
114 The Mall, Pacific Place
88 Queensway, Admiralty
Tel: 2845 4600 and
200 Ocean Terminal, Harbour City, Tsim Sha Tsui.
Tel: 2735 6111
Bustling, 1950s-style American brasserie serving the biggest and best burgers in town. $$–$$$

GADDI'S
1st Floor, The Peninsula Hotel
Salisbury Road, Tsim Sha Tsui
Tel: 2366 6251 ext 3171
Superlative. Deserving all of the accolades it receives for its classic French cooking, wines and service. Reservation and smart dress essential. $$$$

GRISSINI
2nd Floor, The Grand Hyatt Hotel
1 Harbour Road, Wan Chai
Tel: 2588 1234 ext 7313
Mouthwateringly delicious Milanese food, charming service, striking modern interior and spectacular harbour views. A pleasantly relaxed Italian hotel restaurant. $$$–$$$$

HARRY RAMSDEN'S
213 Queen's Road East, Wan Chai
Tel 2832 9626
A cheery retro-nostalgia fish 'n chips restaurant from Yorkshire. Great family-dining with generous portions, and friendly staff. $

Il Mercato
Basement California Entertainment Building, 34–36 D'Aguilar Street, Central
Tel: 2868 3068
Unpretentious Italian trattoria in the heart of trendy Lan Kwai Fong. $$

Yau Ma Tei roast meat shop

Nightlife

Hong Kong has a diverse nightlife menu that reflects its cross-cultural heritage. You can find current entertainment reviews and listings in the English-language press; the two freebies *HK Magazine* and *BC Magazine*; the free HKTA *Essential: The Official Hong Kong Guide* and weekly calendar *Hong Kong Diary*, while the free HKTA *Official Dining, Entertainment and Shopping Guide* gives a broad selection of bars and nightclubs.

Performing Arts

On the cultural front, classical music, jazz, ballet and contemporary dance, which transcend language barriers more easily than theatre, are well-represented. The **Hong Kong Arts and City ('Fringe') Festivals** (early spring) are highlights of the performing arts calendar but there are regular performances by the city's two orchestras (**HK Philharmonic Orchestra** and **HK Chinese Orchestra**) and three professional dance troupes (**HK Ballet Company**, **City Contemporary Dance Company** and **HK Dance Company**), as well as guest appearances by high-calibre overseas artistes, from September through July.

Traditional **Chinese opera** has a strong following locally with troupes performing Chiu Chow, Beijing and Cantonese forms – at different venues on an irregular basis and free of charge – in makeshift theatres erected near temples during major Chinese festivals. While the lyrics aren't really accessible to non-Chinese speakers, the elaborate make-up, sets and costumes are spectacular.

The **Festival of Asian Arts**, held every other year in late autumn, attracts a fascinating blend of traditional and *avant garde* music, dance and theatre from around the region. Hong Kong also enjoys an eclectic celebration of Gallic talent each year in **Le French May**, the biggest French festival in Asia.

Tickets for most cultural events and concerts are sold through the Urban Council's computerised ticketing agency URBTIX (reservations hotline tel: 2734 9009), which has centrally-located outlets at HK Academy for Performing Arts; HK Arts Centre; City Hall; HK Cultural Centre; and Tom Lee Music Shops at 6 Cameron Lane, Tsim Sha Tsui; 521 Hennessy Road, Causeway Bay; and 2nd Floor, City Centre Building, 144–149 Gloucester Road, Wan Chai.

Cultural Centres

ACADEMY FOR PERFORMING ARTS
1 Gloucester Road, Wan Chai
Tel: 2584 8500; box office 2584 8514
College of dance, music and drama that doubles as a performance venue.

BRUCE LEE CAFÉ AT THE RICKSHAW CLUB
22 Robinson Road, Mid-Levels
Tel: 2525 3977
Kitsch and kicks at Hong Kong's only place of tribute to martial arts legend Bruce Lee. In addition to memorabilia and video screenings, fans may get a chance to meet owner Jon Benn, who starred with Lee in *Way of the Dragon*. A tasty menu and salsa nights every Tuesday, Thursday and Saturday draw a wider crowd.

CITY HALL
Low Block, 1 Edinburgh Place, Central
Tel: 2921 2840
The oldest performing arts venue of any importance in the territory with a 1,400-seat concert hall and a 450-seat theatre. The foyer is a good place to find out about – and book tickets for – performances taking place here and at other venues.

FRINGE CLUB
2 Lower Albert Road, Central
Tel: 2521 7251
Alternative arts venue with a lively programme of contemporary acts housed in an old dairy farm building. Studio theatres, contemporary art exhibitions and a bar with live music.

HONG KONG ARTS CENTRE
2 Harbour Road, Wan Chai
Tel: 2582 0200; box office 2582 0232
Compact, high-rise complex with performing arts theatres, art house cinema, visual arts exhibition space, and a pleasant café.

HONG KONG CULTURAL CENTRE
10 Salisbury Road, Tsim Sha Tsui
Tel: 2734 2010
City's premier classical music and dance venue. Home of the Hong Kong Philharmonic Orchestra and the Hong Kong Chinese Orchestra. Boasts a 2,000-seat concert hall and 1,750-seat theatre, studio theatre and large foyer with information on upcoming cultural events throughout the territory, music bookshop, and free concerts most weekend afternoons.

Bars/Clubs/Pubs

BAHAMA MAMA'S COCONUT BAR
4–5 Knutsford Terrace, Tsim Sha Tsui
Tel: 2368 2121
Unpretentious Caribbean-inspired bar with reggae, funk, soul, happy house and Motown sounds and a dance floor.

BIG APPLE PUB & DISCO
Basement, 20 Luard Road, Wan Chai
Tel: 2529 3461
There's nothing sophisticated about this rather downscale dance venue; but the after-hours club scene is hot; and it's been voted the raunchiest singles' nightspot in town for several years now. Cover charge after 9pm.

CALIFORNIA BAR & RESTAURANT
Ground Floor, California Tower
24–26 Lan Kwai Fong, Central
Tel: 2521 1345
The place that put Lan Kwai Fong on the map. Smart, upbeat American bar-cum-restaurant with Tex Mex fare, loud music, video clips and a tiny dance floor.

CARNEGIE'S
53–55 Lockhart Road, Wan Chai
Tel: 2866 6289
Friendly, relaxed bar with American-style eats and a regular clientele who loves to party.

CHAMPAGNE BAR
Lobby, Grand Hyatt Hotel,
1 Harbour Road, Wan Chai
Tel: 2588 1234
Elegant yet intimate art deco setting and top-notch vocals and piano music enhance the sybaritic pleasure of having 39 champagnes to choose from.

CLUB SHANGHAI
Mezzanine Level, Regent Hotel
18 Salisbury Road, Tsim Sha Tsui
Tel: 2721 1211
Upscale yet trendy nightclub recapturing the glamour and panache of nightlife in 1930s Shanghai. Big band classics and upbeat contemporary sounds for listening or dancing.

DELANEY'S
Mary Building, 71–77 Peking Road, Tsim Sha Tsui
Tel: 2301 3980 and
2nd Floor, One Capital Place
18 Luard Road, Wan Chai
Tel: 2804 2880
With fixtures and fittings imported lock, stock and barrel from the Emerald Isle; authentic Irish fare a cut above the average pub-grub; good music; and friendly staff, it's not hard to imagine yourself in a Dublin city pub rather than Hong Kong.

FELIX
28th Floor, The Peninsula Hotel
Salisbury Road, Tsim Sha Tsui
Tel: 2315 3188
Design enthusiasts should put a visit to Philippe Starck's *avant garde* 'brasserie for the 21st century' at the top of their list. It's visual drama, from the elevator ride to Starck's signature furniture and the stunning toilets, plus spectacular views of the Hong Kong skyline. If you can't afford dinner (Pan-Asian cuisine), settle for cocktails or after-dinner drinks.

HARD ROCK CAFÉ
100 Canton Road, Tsim Sha Tsui
Tel: 2736 1101
The tried and tested formula of hearty American fare, cheery service, wicked shakes and cocktails, Top 40 chart music and rock 'n roll memorabilia.

JJ'S
Grand Hyatt Hotel,
1 Harbour Road, Wan Chai
Tel: 2588 1234 ext 7323
Hong Kong's premier nightclub. Two floors of flashy fun with nightly live music. Favourite afterhours playground of affluent executives and bright young things. (Dress code)

JOE BANANAS
23 Luard Road, Wan Chai
Tel: 2529 1811
Smart bar with American-style bistro menu by day and a disco party mood by night. (Dress code)

KARA KARAOKE
Level 3, Convention Plaza
1 Harbour Road, Wan Chai
Tel: 2824 0606
This is an upmarket karaoke bar popular with young executives. Fun on a crowded night.

LA CITÉ
LG1, One Pacific Place
88 Queensway, Admiralty
Tel: 2522 8830
Smart, chic, French bistro with a great sidewalk ambience.

La Dolce Vita 97
9 Lan Kwai Fong, Central
Tel: 2810 8098
Funky open-fronted Italian cafe-bar with pulsating post-house music and delicious Italian snacks. One of the best people-watching spots on the Fong. Stays open late.

Mad Dogs
1 D'Aguilar Street, Central
Tel: 2810 1000
Convivial English pub with period decor, friendly staff, and quality eats.

Ned Kelly's Last Stand
11A Ashley Road, Tsim Sha Tsui
Tel: 2376 0562
Live music and rolicking beery fun are the hallmarks of this goodtime Aussie pub.

Petticoat Lane, The Pavilion and El Pomposo
3–5 Tun Wo Lane, Central
Tel: 2869 7768/2973 0642/ 2869 7679
Vibrant little trio consisting of a funky baroque bar, intimate continental bistro and Spanish tapas bar. Clientele and décor would be right at home in a Pedro Almodovar film. Not cheap but great fun.

Red Rock
Basement, 57–59 Wyndham Street, Central
Tel: 2868 0613
Trendy continental restaurant and bar with boutique beers from around the world and an outside terrace that gets packed on Friday nights. Dancing after 10.30pm.

The Dublin Jack
37–43 Cochrane Street, Central
Tel: 2543 0081
One of the most successful approximations of a period Irish pub in Hong Kong, with an exterior that looks like a traditional Dublin post office and pavement drinking space. Draft Irish beers and single malt whiskies ensure a loyal clientele.

The Jazz and Blues Club & Bar
2nd Floor, California Entertainment Building, 34–36 D'Aguilar Street
Tel: 2845 8477
Live performances from top flight international talents as well as local musicians. Jazz and blues video clips in the adjoining bar area. Cover charge for live performances; book ahead for international acts.

The Jump
7th Level, Causeway Bay Plaza II
463 Lockhart Road, Causeway Bay
Tel: 2832 9007
Festive American-style bar with TexMex fare, Long Island iced tea and beer by the pitcher, an infamous dentist's chair tequila and lime challenge, and dancing after 11pm.

The Nightingale Karaoke Club
2nd Floor, The Charterhouse, 209–19 Wanchai Road
Tel: 2891 1739
International karaoke club where you can book a private room to sing along with friends or join in with other customers in the intimate club lounge. They have a large selection of songs in Chinese, English, French, Japanese and Tagalog (Filipino).

The Wanch
54 Jaffe Road, Wan Chai
Tel: 2861 1621
Well-established live music pub with a good line-up of local talent and regular Wednesday night jam sessions. The Wanch is sometimes loud, sometimes elevating, but never dull.

Shopping

Shoppers are one group to have benefited from Hong Kong's economic downturn. Inflation rates on consumer prices fell to 2.6–3.2 percent at end 1998 (down from 5.7–6.1 percent in 1997 and 8.5–9 percent in 1993). A further 2 percent drop in consumer price inflation is predicted for the 1999–2000 budget year. This translates as bargains galore for Hong Kong shoppers but a testing time for many retailers.

Hong Kong came out tops in terms of offering best value for money on imported luxury leather goods in an April 1999 Asia Pacific-wide survey by the *Asian Wall Street Journal.*

Before you start browsing, pick up a copy of the HKTA's *Official Dining, Entertainment and Shopping Guide* and *Essential: The Official Hong Kong Guide*, two free booklets which offer many useful tips. An important thing to note about shopping in Hong Kong is that goods purchased are not normally returnable or refundable; so don't make expensive purchases if you're not absolutely certain. That said, if you run into any other problems – nasty shop assistants or rip-offs – call the HKTA's multi-lingual hotline at tel: 2508 1234. If the offending shop is a HKTA member, the tourist board will try to resolve the matter. Otherwise, it can recommend cases to the Hong Kong Consumer Council (tel: 2929 2222). So remember, tourists do have some clout in Hong Kong.

Fashion

Hong Kong tailors are as skilled as ever; both at classic tailoring and copying existing garments. Prices vary according to the work involved as well as the quality and quantity of cloth and trimmings. You can get a good custom-tailored shirt for about HK$250 and a suit for about HK$2,300. Quality tailors prefer you to allow time for a couple of fittings; the so-called 24-hour suit at rock bottom prices is rarely the bargain it sounds. **Tailor Kwan (Creative)** and **Yuen's Tailors** (both in the Central Escalator Link Alley on the 2nd Floor of Central Market), **Sam's Tailor** (Burlington Arcade K, 92–94 Nathan Road, Tsim Sha Tsui) and **William Cheng & Son** (8th Floor, 38 Hankow Road, Tsim Sha Tsui) are recommended.

Designer boutiques invaded Hong Kong during the 1980s, primarily to serve the locals and Japanese tourists. All the big names

Gucci, one of many designer labels in HK

are here – Armani, Chanel, DKNY, Issey Miyake and dozens more. They cluster in **The Landmark**, **Pacific Place**, **Prince's Building** and **Times Square** on Hong Kong-side; the top-flight hotel arcades, **New World Centre** and **Harbour City** complex, and along **Canton Road** in Tsim Sha Tsui. Upscale department stores **Lane Crawford** and **Seibu**, and local fashion moguls **Joyce** and **The Swank Shop**, stock many designer labels under one roof. Don't expect lower prices than in Europe or US.

However, you can get good deals on world-renowned Hong Kong-based **Diane Freis** fashions and **Marguerite Lee** lingerie; as well as fashions by home-grown talents like Lu Lu Cheung, Allan Chiu, Anna Sui, Vivienne Tam and Walter Ma. Inspiring work by up-and-coming Hong Kong designers can be found in the **TDC Design Gallery** (Level 1, Convention Plaza, Harbour Road, Wan Chai). More unusual still are quintessential Chinese cheongsams, Mao suits and Tang jackets available off-the-peg or custom-tailored from **Shanghai Tang** (Pedder Building).

Low- to middle-range fashion chains have outlets in every shopping district, with international brand names competing with locally-produced labels like Bossini Colour Eighteen, Giordano, Episode, Jessica and U2.

For real bargains, head for the street markets and factory outlets. For a fraction of the price back home, these sell samples, over-runs and slightly damaged 'seconds' of locally-manufactured clothes designed for the export market. As a general guide, bargain-priced womenswear, menswear, T-shirts and jeans, and children's clothes can be found in the **factory outlets** along **Haiphong** and **Granville** roads in Tsim Sha Tsui; **Spring Garden Lane** and **Johnston Road** in Wan Chai; **Jardine's Crescent** and **Lee Garden Road** in Causeway Bay; **Stanley Market**; and **Tung Choi Street Ladies' Market** and **Fa Yuen Street** in Mong Kok. The shops in the **Pedder Building**, Central, are good places to look for quality womenswear and **Temple Street Night Market** has cheap menswear. The usual *caveat emptor* ruling applies as not all of the so-called designer label merchandise is genuine.

Electronics & Photographic Equipment

If you're prepared to shop around, this is another area where you can still find cut-rate prices in Hong Kong. Shops selling televisions, video cam-

Kowloon camera shop

Checking equipment

eras and recorders, DVD/VCD/MD players, stereo systems, and portable tape and CD players cluster in **Causeway Bay** and **Tsim Sha Tsui**, and especially along Nathan, Peking, Mody and Carnarvon roads in Tsim Sha Tsui. Be warned that some dealers in the major tourist areas employ unscrupulous methods. Compare prices, resist pressure sales tactics and always check the goods and receipt before leaving the shop. If in doubt, stick to merchants listed in the *HKTA Official Dining, Entertainment and Shopping Directory*. The fixed-price retail chains **Broadway Photo Supply** and **Fortress** are good alternatives if you don't enjoy haggling.

Computer equipment can be found at the **Computer Mall** in Windsor House, Causeway Bay; **Star Computer City** in Star House and the **Silvercord Centre** in Tsim Sha Tsui; **Mongkok Computer Centre** and **Golden Shopping Centre** in Sham Shui Po. A wide range of hardware and software are available, but prices for genuine PCs and programmes are about the same as in Europe and the US. The government is cracking down on pirated software and visitors are advised to stick to legitimate purchases.

The streets around Nathan Road are also chockful of camera shops. But most local professional photographers buy their film and equipment on Hong Kong-side, at **Photo Scientific Appliances** (6 Stanley Street, Central).

Art, Antiques, Handicrafts & Furniture

Hong Kong is a centre for Asian arts and crafts, with museum-quality antique furniture, ceramics, sculptures, textiles and traditional paintings from China, Tibet, Japan, and southeast Asia. More affordable are modern Chinese and Vietnamese paintings, Oriental rugs, reproduction Korean chests, 'antique' Chinese furniture and ceramics, Thai Buddha figurines, Balinese woodwork, Chinese folk paintings and other ethnic crafts.

The greatest concentration of antique and carpet dealers is along **Hollywood Road** and **Upper Wyndham Street** in Central, but there are also a number of top quality shops in **Pacific Place**, and at

Hollywood Road figurine

Harbour City and **New World Centre** on Kowloon-side. Fine art galleries are more spread out still so it's best to check under exhibition listings in the newspapers, or in the free HKTA *Hong Kong Diary, BC* and *HK Magazine*.

The **Chinese Arts & Crafts (HK) Ltd**, **CRC Department Store** and **Yue Hwa Chinese Products Emporium** are great places to look for Chinese arts and crafts; while shops like **Amazing Grace Elephant Co** (Harbour City, Tsim Sha Tsui), **The Banyan Tree** (Prince's Building, Central; Harbour City and Horizon Plaza, Ap Lei Chau), **Tequila Kola** (United Centre, Admiralty and Horizon Plaza, Ap Lei Chau), **Vincent Sum Collection** (Lyndhurst Terrace, Central) and **Mountain Folkcraft** (Wo On Lane, Central) stock furniture and craft items from elsewhere in Asia. **Welfare Handicrafts** in Jardine House in Central or the **Hong Kong Museum of Art Gift Shop** are good places to pick up smaller gift items and cards; **Alan Chan Creations** in the Peak Galleria offers stylishly nostalgic graphic design items by one of Hong Kong's leading design gurus.

Queen's Road East in Wan Chai is the best place for customised rattan and reproduction rosewood furniture. For keener prices on Chinese and Asian antiques and contemporary furnishings/lifestyle items, it's worth checking out the wholesale import/export outlets in Aberdeen. These are conveniently concentrated in two warehouse buildings: the **Hing Wai Centre**, No 7 Tin Wan Praya Road, and **Horizon Plaza**, No 2 Lee Wing Street, Ap Lei Chau. While you're there, you might want to check out the Chinese ceramics produced by local factory **Wah Tung China** in the Grand Marine Industrial Building, No 3 Yue Fung Street, Shek Pai Wan (it also has a small outlet on Hollywood Road).

Queen's Road gold shop

Jewellery, Watches & Gemstones

Hong Kong is the world's largest jade market, the third largest diamond trading centre after New York and Antwerp, one of the largest gold brokers, and a magnet for precious stones from all over Asia, and pearls from the Pacific Rim. Many finished jewellery items are manufactured in Hong Kong, these can range from simple gold bangles to exquisite and intricate diamond necklaces.

A lot of people think they get the best buys on gold and jewellery at factory outlets in Hung Hom. But these have been flooded with bus loads of Japanese tourists in recent years and prices have risen accordingly. Better bargains, in fact, can be found in the jewellery and gold shops along **Queen's Road Central**. **Chinese Arts & Crafts**, **CRC Department Store** and **Yue Hwa Chinese Products Emporium** offer good deals on gold and jade with a written guarantee. Top-flight hotel shopping arcades are another place that you can find quality jewellers.

It's always a good idea to get a professional gemologist to certify authenticity before you purchase diamonds, jade or other gemstones. Contact the HK Gemological Society at tel: 2366 6006.

Designer watch shops selling the top brands cluster along the lower end of Nathan Road in Kowloon – which is equally famous for sleazy 'copy-watch' salesmen – and in the malls of Central. **City Chain** is a reasonably-priced watch retailer with more than 40 branches in Hong Kong. Lots of watches are for sale at the **Temple Street Market** but be warned: they are fakes.

Optical Goods

Hong Kong is a great place to buy eye-wear, whether it's prescription lenses or the latest designer sun-glasses – more than half the population wear spectacles or contact lenses. Designer sun-glasses, frames, lenses and contacts cost considerably less than you'd pay in most other countries; eye-tests are free, and the service is quick and efficient. The largest retail opticians are **Optical 88** (nearly 68 outlets) and **The Optical Shop** (38 outlets) but there are hundreds of smaller opticians to choose from – **Fox Optical** (12 Cochrane Street, Central) and **Mandarin Optical** (79 Queen's Road, Central) are both recommended. **Bunn's Diving Equipment** (No 2 Johnston Road, Wan Chai) sells competitively-priced swimming-goggles and diving masks specially fitted with lenses for people who suffer from myopia.

Tsim Sha Tsui for shopping

Food, Toiletries & Drugs

Traditional fresh produce markets and Chinese dried foodstuff shops all over Hong Kong are worth visiting, if only to look at the exotic foodstuffs. It's also well worth visiting one of the speciality tea shops like **Fook Ming Tong** (The Landmark, Central and Shop 124 Ocean Terminal) or **Lock Cha** (Ladder Street, Central and Citylink Plaza, Sha Tin) as canisters of fragrant Chinese tea make great gift items.

More prosaic food-shopping can be done at the numerous **Wellcome** as well as **Park 'N Shop** supermarkets throughout the territory which stock both Western and Chinese food. **Oliver's Delicatessen**

(Prince's Building, Central and Ocean Centre, Tsim Sha Tsui), **CitySuper** (Times Square, Causeway Bay and Harbour City extension, Tsim Sha Tsui) and **Seibu Food Hall** (Pacific Place) stock imported produce but are more expensive; **Health Gate** (8th floor, 106–8 Des Voeux Road, Central) is a good option for health foods.

Watson's is the largest retail chain specialising in toiletries and drugs, with **Mannings** a close second. **Fanda Perfume** (Worldwide House, Central and 60A Nathan Road, Tsim Sha Tsui) has competitive prices on a wide range of international perfumes and cosmetics; **The Body Shop** and **Red Earth** with their environmentally-friendly products have had franchises here for several years now.

Department Stores

Hong Kong's oldest department store **Lane Crawford** and the upmarket Japanese store **Seibu** in **Pacific Place** are the local equivalents of Bloomingdale's or Harrod's – classy and very expensive. For more down-to-earth prices, try the other long-established local department stores like **Sincere** and **Wing On**, where the local people go to shop.

The Japanese department stores in Causeway Bay – **Sogo** and **Mitsukoshi** (Seibu also has a Causeway Bay branch) – are very popular with both local Hong Kongers as well as the Japanese expatriate community. Likewise, the several branches of **Marks & Spencer** are a little piece of Britain in the tropics (pricier than in the UK).

However, it's the fascinating mainland Chinese department store chains that are most worthy of exploration, even if you don't intend to buy: **Chinese Arts & Crafts (HK) Ltd**, **Yue Hwa Chinese Products Emporium** and **CRC Department Stores**. Finally, don't miss the local-owned designer-chic 1930s-style **Shanghai Tang** department store (Pedder Building, Central). It has great retro-nostalgia Chinese fashions and gift items.

Pacific Place for upmarket shopping

Calendar of Special Events

JANUARY – FEBRUARY

The calendar starts with a public holiday on **New Year's Day**, 1 January. But things don't start swinging until Lunar or **Chinese New Year** in late January or early February. This is the most joyous time of the year in Hong Kong, when buildings are festooned with colourful lights and decorations. Bouquets of chrysanthemums, peach blossoms and *kumquat* trees are sold in markets, and bright red *lai see* packets containing money are handed out to children and unmarried adults. A big family dinner is held on Lunar New Year's Eve. The next day, people flock to Chinese temples to make offerings of joss sticks, food and paper money. A huge fireworks display is staged over Victoria Harbour as millions of people line the shore. Don't forget to say: *Kung Hay Fat Choi* – Wishing You Prosperity.

Chinese New Year banner

January is a good month for contemporary arts lovers as the **City Festival** organised by the Fringe Club offers an eclectic programme of local and international performers and art shows. The **Hong Kong Arts Festival** also takes place from late February to mid March. Famous singers, musicians, actors and dancers come from all around the globe to perform at venues like the Cultural Centre and the Academy for Performing Arts.

MARCH – APRIL

Hong Kong's top international sporting event is the **Rugby Sevens**, which takes place in late March at Hong Kong Stadium. The **Hong Kong International Film Festival** in April is a cinematic feast for the territory's film buffs. In the same month is the **Hong Kong Food Festival**.

The main Chinese festival during the spring season is **Ching Ming**. In April, the living honour their ancestors by cleaning their graves and making offerings.

MAY – JUNE

Chinese fishermen worship Tin Hau, the patron goddess of the sea, who is honoured

Bun Festival display

by the **Tin Hau Festival** in May (occasionally in April). Hundreds of junks, sampans and trawlers bearing shrines and colourful banners cruise to Tin Hau temples at Joss House Bay and Po Toi Island.

Not long after is the **Bun Festival**

Dragon Boat competition

on Cheung Chau Island, one of Hong Kong's most unusual and photogenic celebrations. The intent is to pacify restless ghosts who are said to roam the island. The week-long festival culminates with processions in which village children are dressed in elaborate costumes and lifted into the air on wooden platforms.

Summer is ushered in by the **Dragon Boat Festival**, which is actually two events on consecutive weekends. Local dragon boat races are staged on the first weekend, with competitions staged at various venues around the colony including Aberdeen Harbour, Sha Tin and Stanley Main Beach. A few days later are the International Dragon Boat Races at the Shing Mun River at Sha Tin, featuring teams from around the Pacific.

JULY – AUGUST

It's hot and steamy during the Hong Kong summer, but the heat doesn't stop Chinese devotees from trying to placate lost souls during the **Hungry Ghost Festival**, or Yue Lan, in August by burning paper offerings.

SEPTEMBER – OCTOBER

The **Mid-Autumn** or **Lantern Festival** (also called the Mooncake Festival) is a magical, mystical September evening when lanterns and candles adorn nearly every park, public square and beach in Hong Kong. Some are elaborate creations in the form of dragons, lions and other mythical creatures, but modern designs are now common including aeroplanes, ships and cars. Best places to watch are Statue Square and Chater Garden in Central, Victoria Park in Causeway Bay and Repulse Bay Beach.

Local punters mark September on their calendars because the **racing season** at Sha Tin and Happy Valley kicks off this month. October features the **Cheung Yung Festival**, another occasion for cleaning graves.

NOVEMBER – DECEMBER

Some of the fastest cars and motorbikes in the world take to the streets of Macau in November on a weekend of racing at the **Macau Grand Prix**.

The majority might be Buddhist, but the people of Hong Kong have taken to **Christmas** in a big way. The run-up to 25 December is marked by splashy light displays and yule decorations throughout Hong Kong.

Check with the Hong Kong Tourist Association (tel: 2508 1234) for festival or event dates and information on tickets or special package tours.

Christmas light-up

Practical Information

GETTING THERE

By Air

Hong Kong is served by dozens of airlines and the world's biggest airport terminal. Opened in July 1998, Chek Lap Kok International Airport is a state-of-the-art facility designed by British architect Sir Norman Foster and covering 550,000sq m of reclaimed land on the north shore of Lantau Island.

The airport is open 24 hours a day and is easily accessed from Hong Kong Island and Kowloon (see *To and From the Airport*). There are 54 moving walkways and an internal shuttle train between the East and West halls to cut down on walking, and multiple immigration and customs desks keep waits to a minimum. And, as this is Hong Kong, shopping opportunities abound in the airport's 30,000sq m Sky Mall. A variety of food and beverage outlets can be found in the Sky Mall and the Regal Airport Hotel next door to the passenger terminal. There is a departure tax of HK$50 for passengers 12 years old and above.

Airport enquiry hotline: 2181 0000.

TRAVEL ESSENTIALS

When to Visit

The ideal period is October through December when the climate is at its finest, with mild temperatures, blue skies and low humidity.

Chinese New Year offers a spectacular fireworks display over Victoria Harbour and other festivities, but many shops and restaurants close over the three public holidays, and flights in and out of Hong Kong are booked up months in advance.

The rainy season, and the sticky heat of the summer generally make March to August the least pleasant months for walking about – but it's a great time for experiencing traditional Chinese festivals and international events such as the Hong Kong Film Festival and Rugby Sevens (see *Calendar of Special Events*).

Visas

Most visitors only need a valid passport to enter Hong Kong. The length of visa-free tourist visit allowed varies according to nationality. British subjects holding full UK passports are granted 6 months upon entry. All other European Union nationals get 3 months; as do most British dependent passport holders; and nationals of Australia, Brazil, Brunei, Chile, Equador, Israel, Malaysia, New Zealand, Norway, Japan, Singapore, Switzerland, Turkey and the USA. Nationals of Argentina, Iceland, Morocco, South Africa, Thailand, Tunisia, Venezuela get 1 month. Nationals of Bangladesh, India, Indonesia and the Philippines get 14 days. Other nationals should consult the Chinese Embassy or Consulate General in their country of origin; or the Immigration Department in Hong Kong, prior to their visit. Note that passports should be valid at least one month beyond the planned date of departure.

Anyone wishing to stay longer than the visa-free period is advised to apply for a visa before travelling to Hong Kong. A tourist visa does not allow you to take up work, study or establish or join any business in Hong Kong.

For information on visa extensions, call the Hong Kong Immigration Department's 24-hour recorded information hotline, tel: 2824 6111. Current information about visa, immigration and entry requirements can also be obtained from the Hong Kong Immigration Department Homepage <http://www.info.gov.hk/immd/english/topical/e/1.htm> or from the Hong Kong Tourist Association's Infofax service and Homepage (see *Tourist Information*).

Hong Kong residents are required to carry an identity card. To avoid any possible confusion, visitors are advised to carry at all times a similar form of photo identification, such as a passport.

Health

No vaccinations are required to enter Hong Kong. Visitors are advised to take out adequate travel and health insurance before leaving their home country to cover hospitalisation and medical expenses in case of accident or sickness. Hong Kong does not have a free national health care system and all medical treatment must be paid for, except for initial emergency treatment at a public hospital.

Hong Kong's air quality has deteriorated in recent years, and asthma sufferers may find themselves affected by atmospheric pollution, particularly in Causeway Bay and Mongkok.

Customs

Hong Kong mostly lives up to its image of being a free port. Visitors aged 18 and above can import just about anything for their personal use (including an unlimited amount of cash) but there are limits on 200 cigarettes (or 50 cigars/250g of tobacco) and one litre of wine or spirits.

If you carry firearms they must be declared and handed over for safe-keeping until you depart. There are also stringent restrictions on the import and export of ivory and other items from endangered species protected by CITES (Convention on International Trade in Endangered Species of Wild Fauna and Flora).

Climate

Hong Kong is situated just south of the tropic of Cancer and has a sub-tropical climate divided into four seasons:

Winter: Between late December and February, the weather generally varies from mild to cool with some fog and rain. Temperatures average between 13°C (55°F) to 20°C (68°F). However, it can occasionally dip down to near freezing for short spells.

Spring: The period from March to mid-May is usually dominated by wet, overcast weather. You can go for days without seeing the sun or blue skies; although there have been some exceptionally fine days during this period in recent years. Temperatures range from a daytime average of 19°C (66°F) in March to 28°C (83°F) in May; humidity averages 77 percent.

Summer: Temperatures and humidity rise to almost unbearable levels from late-May to mid-September as the southwest monsoon blows in from equatorial Asia. Skies are intermittently clear, but generally hazy. Temperatures can easily rise to 35°C (95°F) in the afternoon, with humidity topping 86 percent. Thunderstorms are common, and July–September is also the peak typhoon period.

Autumn/Fall: The northeast monsoon takes over, bringing cooler, drier air from Central Asia. From late-September through December expect clear blue skies and mild temperatures ranging between 18°C (64°F) and 29°C (84°F). The average humidity drops to 72 percent.

Clothing

Appropriate attire depends on the season. During the hot months May–October pack light cotton clothing. Shorts, T-shirts and comfortable shoes or sandals are essential, especially if you're going to be spending a lot of time outdoors.

Temperatures can vary dramatically from one day to the next from November through April, and you should pack accordingly, for both warm and cool climes. The 'strip theory' is best: dress in layers that can be peeled off or put back on according to temperature shifts. A light sweater, umbrella and/or raincoat are highly recommended. Few buildings have heating so during a cold spell it can often seem colder inside than out.

'Smart casual' attire will see you comfortably through most social occasions, outside of business (when suits or dresses are the standard attire) or high-society functions. If you plan on eating at one of the more elegant restaurants, something on the more formal side is best. Be warned: some hotels, restaurants, bars and nightclubs will not admit patrons in sneakers, flip-flops (thongs), jeans or shorts; or collar-less shirts (for men).

Contact lens wearers unaccustomed to air-conditioning (most restaurants, offices, shopping malls and the MTR are notoriously cold, even on the hottest summer's day) may experience some irritation; spectacles, and some hard contact lenses, tend to mist up as you move from cold interiors to sultry outdoors.

Electricity

Electrical outlets in Hong Kong are rated at 200/220 volts and 50 cycles AC (alternating current). Most hotels can supply all-purpose adapters.

When purchasing electronics (DVDs, TVs, VCDs, VCRs and music systems) in Hong Kong, be sure to get a system that matches your broadcasting system and voltage back home.

Time

Hong Kong is eight hours ahead of GMT and 13 hours ahead of Eastern Standard Time in the US.

GETTING ACQUAINTED

Geography

Hong Kong packs over 6.8 million people into an area of 1,097sq km/424sq miles (a figure which continues to grow because of land reclamation). It is one of the most crowded places on earth, with a density of 6,206 people per sq km. Mong Kok district in Kowloon and the new town development of Kwun Tong (home to over 54,000 people per sq km) are thought to be two of the world's most densely populated urban areas. What is perhaps less well known is that protected country parks make up over 40 percent of the territory.

The territory is divided into four main areas: Hong Kong Island, Kowloon, the New Territories and the Outlying Islands (although these are officially part of the New Territories). Its most valuable natural features are its deep-water harbour and anchorages.

Hong Kong Island has been the seat of both government and financial power in the territory since the British took possession in 1841. It is home to more than 1.45 million people, most of whom live along the coast. The middle of the island is dominated by Victoria Peak (554m/1,817ft) and other mountains.

Across Victoria Harbour is the tightly-packed Kowloon peninsula, which was ceded (along with Stonecutters' Island) from China in 1860 and is now home to more than 2 million people. Beyond Boundary Street is the vast area called the New Territories, which was leased to Britain for 99 years in 1898, along with 233 Outlying Islands. Giant 'new towns' have sprung up at Kwun Tong, Ma On Shan, Sha Tin, Tai Po, Tin Shui Wai, Tsuen Wan, Tuen Mun and Yeun Long since the 1970s, but much of the area remains undeveloped. Tai Mo Shan, the highest point in Hong Kong at 957m (3,139ft), is in the New Territories.

The Outlying Islands comprise 233 separate pieces of land, ranging in size from mere rocks to giant Lantau which is more than twice the size of Hong Kong Island. Except for Cheung Chau, the Outlying Islands are generally sparsely populated with large open areas, high mountains and isolated bays and beaches. The construction of rail and road links to Chek Lap Kok International Airport via the Tsing Ma Bridge (Hong Kong's 'Golden Gate') connected Lantau to the Kowloon peninsula for the first time in 1998 and the island is experiencing major changes.

Language

Hong Kong's official languages are Chinese and English. Street names, public transport and utilities signage, and government publications are bilingual, as are most notices, signage and menus.

The predominant spoken language of street level Hong Kong is Cantonese

(*Guandonghua*), a regional Chinese dialect that is also spoken in Guangdong province in China. It's a tonal language and very difficult for the uninitiated to pronounce. The use of Mandarin Chinese (*Putonghua*) is on the increase and has become increasingly prevalent after the handover in July 1997. For the moment, however, English is still the language of international business and most people who come into contact with tourists speak at least a smidgen of English. With taxi drivers it's sometimes a different story. It's best to have your destination written down in Chinese characters by a friend or someone at the hotel front desk. Another handy trick is to carry a printed card with the name of your hotel in Chinese. That way you can always get back to where you started from.

Cantonese and Mandarin phrasebooks can be purchased at most bookstores; *The Right Word in Cantonese* by Kwan Choi Wah (Commercial Press, Hong Kong) is a handy quick reference vocabulary with a glossary of useful Hong Kong place names, words and phrases.

MONEY MATTERS

Currency

The currency unit is the Hong Kong Dollar, pegged loosely to the US Dollar at a rate of roughly US$1 to HK$7.80.

Bank notes are issued by Hongkong Bank (HSBC), Standard Chartered Bank and the Bank of China. They come in the following denominations: HK$1,000 (orange), HK$500 (brown), HK$100 (red), HK$50 (purple) and HK$20 (green, except for the Bank of China's which are blue). A few old HK$10 (light green) notes are still in circulation. Coins include HK$10, HK$5, HK$2, HK$1, and 50 cents, 20 cents and 10 cents.

Cheques and Credit Cards

Personal cheques are rarely accepted unless you have a local Hong Kong Dollar account. However, traveller's cheques are readily accepted by banks, hotels and money changers. Plastic is used in Hong Kong with a vengeance: Visa, MasterCard, American Express, Diner's Club and other major credit cards are accepted at most hotels, restaurants and shops. Be sure to check the cash price in shops; it may be lower. In most street markets, only cash is accepted. Most establishments which accept credit cards are honest but it's always a good idea to insert the HK$ currency symbol immediately in front of the amount and keep the customer's copy for personal records.

Money Changers

The best places to change foreign currency and traveller's cheques into Hong Kong Dollars are banks – they generally offer the best rates – although most charge non-account holders a commission on all transactions. Banking hours are from 9am–4.30pm Monday to Friday and 9am–12.30pm on Saturday. Licensed money-changers and hotels are an alternative option, but they can sting you with a hefty service charge. Ask about commissions before the transaction. Money-changers in Tsim Sha Tsui, Causeway Bay and Wan Chai are open until late at night.

Cash Machines

Visa and MasterCard holders can obtain local currency from Hang Seng Bank and Hongkong Bank (HSBC) automatic teller machines (ATMs); American Express cardholders can access Jetco ATMs. Wing Lung Bank operates a 24-hour automatic currency exchange called EA$YXCHANGE at its 4 Carnarvon Road (Tsim Sha Tsui) and Shop 101 Convention Centre (Wan Chai) branches.

Remember to take your passport along as identification for traveller's cheques or drawing cash advances on credit cards across the counter.

Tipping

This is not a town for heavy tippers. Most restaurants and hotels automatically add a 10 percent service charge. It's general practice to round up a restaurant bill to the nearest ten (larger gratuities are expected when there is no service charge added onto the bill) or a taxi fare to the nearest dollar or two.

Restroom attendants and doormen can

be tipped one or two dollars. A HK$10–20 is good enough for bellboys and room service in most hotels.

GETTING AROUND

To and From the Airport

The fastest way to get to and from Chek Lap Kok is by the high-speed Airport Express Line (AEL) railway, which links the airport to Hong Kong station in Central in just 23 minutes, with stops at Tsing Yi (12 minutes) and Kowloon station near Tsim Sha Tsui (19 minutes). Tickets to and from Hong Kong station cost HK$70 for single/day return; HK$120 for a return ticket valid for one month; to and from Kowloon station cost HK$60 and HK$100, respectively. Trains depart every 10 minutes, 6–1am daily.

Airport Express passengers can take free shuttle bus transfers between the Hong Kong and Kowloon stations and 21 major hotels, the KCR station at Hung Hom and the China Ferry Terminal. MTR underground railway connections at Tsing Yi and Hong Kong station provide access to other areas of Hong Kong and Kowloon.

A cheaper but slower alternative is to take the ordinary MTR line to Tung Chung (HK$23) and a shuttle bus to the airport.

If you prefer to travel by bus, there are eight Airbus and 22 conventional franchised bus routes to choose from. Average journey time is about one hour and tickets vary from HK$20 to HK$45. Bus services operate around-the-clock.

Taxis are readily available in either direction. At the airport taxi pick-up area, they are zoned according to the area they serve (red for urban Kowloon and Hong Kong; green for the New Territories and blue for Lantau Island). Approximate costs in each direction are HK$330 for Central and HK$270 for Tsim Sha Tsui, including bridge and tunnel fees.

Anyone heading for Tuen Mun or Discovery Bay can also take advantage of the only ferry services out of Chek Lap Kok (for enquiries, tel: 2987 7351).

In town check-in counters for all airlines are located at Hong Kong and Kowloon Airport Express stations; you are advised to check-in two hours before flight departure. The service is free for Airport Express passengers (Airport Express enquiries hotline, tel: 2881 8888).

Taxis

Licensed taxis are available around-the-clock, even in some of the more remote parts of the city. Taxis are zoned and identified by three colours: red for Hong Kong Island and urban Kowloon; green for the New Territories; and blue for Lantau Island. However, taxis do not pick up or set down on yellow lines; and empty taxis are an endangered species during rainstorms, rush hour and the daily shift change at 4pm. Most people queue up for taxis, but in the absence of a taxi stand, it can often deteriorate into an elbow- and briefcase-wielding free-for-all.

At time of writing, the flag fall for red urban taxis is HK$15 for the first 2 km, with a meter that ticks over at HK$1.40 for each additional 0.2 km or minute of waiting time. There are extra charges for tunnel tolls (HK$20 for the Cross Harbour Tunnel; HK$30 for the Eastern Harbour Tunnel; HK$45 for the Western Harbour Tunnel; HK$30 for the Lantau Link; HK$3–8 for other tunnels) and for booked calls, luggage stored in the trunk or boot and luggage handling. Receipts for taxi fares are available on request. The green taxis in the New Territories and the blue taxis on Lantau charge slightly lower fares. All taxis can go to the Hong Kong International Airport at Chek Lap Kok. If you have problems with a taxi driver, make a note of the taxi number (displayed with the driver's name on the dashboard) and call the police hotline, tel: 2527 7177.

Urban (red) taxi paging services – tel: 2527 8524; 2571 2929; 2776 7885.

MTR (Mass Transit Railway)

This underground railway network carries 2.5 million passengers each day. The trains are fast, air-conditioned and efficient. Four inter-connecting lines serve the north side of Hong Kong Island, Kowloon, the southern fringe of the New Territories, Tsing Yi and Tung Chung on Lantau Island. The MTR connects with the high-speed Airport Express Line at Hong Kong station and Tsing Yi; and with the KCR overland railway at Kowloon Tong. The MTR is the fastest way to cross Victoria Harbour between Kowloon and Hong Kong Island.

The MTR operates from 6am to 1am daily. It is best avoided at morning and evening rush hours when there is a terrific crush of bodies. Purchase your tickets before entering the station turnstiles; the automatic ticket machines accept HK$10 coins down to 50-cent coins. Adult single fares range from HK$4 to HK$26. Individual tickets are only valid for the day of issue.

Visitors staying more than a few days might find it worthwhile to buy an Octopus stored-value card which allows you to travel on the Airport Express, MTR, KCR, LRT and some buses and ferries at slightly lower fares. Octopus cards can be purchased at customer service counters at Airport Express and MTR stations. The minimum price is HK$150 which includes a HK$50 deposit (refundable from Airport Express and MTR station customer service counters). For Octopus enquiries, tel: 2993 8880.

Entrances to MTR stations are signposted. There are clear directions in English and Chinese characters inside the stations and the system is easy to navigate once you master one basic concept: namely, that MTR platforms are signposted according to the final station in each direction rather than by the respective line. For instance, the Island Line platform heading west is labelled Sheung Wan and the Island Line heading east is labelled Chai Wan. Consult the MTR map (see page 105) and check which direction you want to go in, the name of the terminus station and relevant interchange stations. Each stop and interchange station is announced in Cantonese and English.

Note that there are no toilet facilities at any of the stations, or on the trains. Smoking is forbidden, and you are not supposed to eat, drink or take large pieces of luggage onto the MTR (with the exception of the Airport Express Line).

For enquiries call the MTR passenger information hotline, tel: 2881 8888.

KCR (Kowloon-Canton Railway)

This track could be the start of an epic rail journey that will take you all the way from the tip of the Kowloon peninsula, across China, the CIS and on to western Europe, Paris or London (providing you sort out red tape and visas in advance).

However, for most tourists and Hong Kong residents, the KCR is a fast and cheap overground railway system linking Kowloon with various outposts in the New Territories such as Sha Tin, Tai Po Market, Fanling and Sheung Shui. It continues to the border crossing at Lo Wu but this is a restricted area and visas are required for China. You can board the KCR at its terminus in Hung Hom and at Mong Kok station, but for many passengers, Kowloon Tong station is more convenient because of its interchange with the MTR.

The KCR is a good way to see the New Territories and the fares are a bargain: the longest journey between Hung Hom and Sheung Shui will set you back HK$9 (ordinary class) or HK$18 (first class); it costs slightly less if you use an Octopus stored-value card (see *MTR*) and children under 12 travel half-price while under-3s travel free. For enquiries call the KCR hotline, tel: 2602 7799.

Ferries

Hong Kong boasts an extensive array of water transport.

The famous green-and-white Star Ferries have been cruising the harbour between Hong Kong Island and Kowloon since 1898. There are 12 ferries in the fleet, all named after celestial entities. The fare between Central and Tsim Sha Tsui is just HK$2.20 for the upper deck and HK$1.70 for the lower deck; the service runs between 6.30am and 11.30pm. The journey takes about 8 minutes and offers one of the most spectacular views of Hong Kong. Other Star Ferries ply routes between Central and Hung Hom (for Kowloon Railway station) and between Tsim Sha Tsui and Wan Chai (for the Hong Kong Convention and Exhibition Centre). For enquiries call Star Ferry Holdings Co, tel: 2366 2576.

Passenger ferries to the Outlying Islands (Cheung Chau, Lamma, Lantau and Peng Chau), Tsing Yi and Tsuen Wan leave from the Central Ferry Piers on the waterfront on the reclaimed land in front of Exchange Square and Hong Kong station (to the west of the Star Ferry Concourse in Central).

Ferries to Cheung Chau leave from Pier 6 and ferries to Lantau (Mui Wo) and Peng Chau leave from Pier 7, and are operated by the Hong Kong & Yau Ma Tei Ferry Co (HKF). For enquiries, call tel: 2542 3081. Ferries to Lamma, Tsing Yi and Tsuen Wan leave from Pier 5 and are operated by the Hong Kong Kowloon Ferry (HKKF). For details, call tel: 2815 6063. HKKF operates two services to Lamma, so be sure to check whether you want Yung Shue Wan or Sok Kwu Wan before you board.

The ferries are increasingly high-speed vessels or hoverferries, but HKF still operates slower 'ordinary ferries' to Cheung Chau and Lantau. These sturdy black-and-white vessels offer spectacular views of the crowded anchorage in the outer harbour for a fraction of the price of an organised tour.

Fares range from HK$10 on weekdays to HK$30 for a Sunday or holiday crossing on a fast ferry or HK$24 for the air-conditioned 'deluxe' deck on triple deck vessels (which has the added advantage of a sundeck at the back). It's advisable to allow time for ticket queues during peak commuter-hours, weekends and public holidays. For details call ferry schedule hotline, tel: 2525 1108 (24 hours); HKF customer service hotline, tel: 2542 3081 (8am–6pm).

Discovery Bay, a residential development on Lantau, has its own ferry service from Central (HK$25 each way) and also operates ferries between Central and Tsim Sha Tsui East; between Chek Lap Kok and Tuen Mun; and between Chek Lap Kok and Discovery Bay. At the time of writing, ferries leave from the east side of the Star Ferry in Central; they are eventually scheduled to depart from Pier 3 of the Central Ferry Piers. For information, tel: 2987 7351.

You can also catch jetfoils, catamarans, hoverferries and high-speed ferries to the Portuguese enclave of Macau (60km/37 miles) west of Hong Kong, from the Macau Ferry Terminal in the Shun Tak Centre, 200 Connaught Road, Central (Sheung Wan MTR) or the China Ferry Terminal at 33 Canton Road in Tsim Sha Tsui (for further information contact the Macau Government Tourist Office at Shop 336 in the Shun Tak Centre, tel: 2857 2287). There are also a variety of scheduled boat services to Guangzhou and other destinations in mainland China from these ferry teminals (for further information, contact China Travel Services (CTS) on tel: 2853 3888).

Buses

Hong Kong has a variety of bus services. Large single and double-decker buses are operated by Citybus (tel: 2873 0818) and New World First Bus (tel: 2136 8888) on Hong Kong Island, Kowloon and the New Territories; by Kowloon Motor Bus (KMB; tel: 2745 4466); and by the New Lantao Bus Co (tel: 2984 9848) on Lantau island.

Fares range from HK$1.20 for short journeys in the city to HK$45 for longer trips into the New Territories. You drop the fare into a box as you enter and no change is given so it's a good idea to keep plenty of small change handy. Some buses also accept Octopus stored-value cards (see *MTR*). Final destinations are marked in English and Chinese on the front top panel. Drivers rarely speak much English.

Minibuses (pale yellow with a red stripe) and maxicabs (pale yellow with a green stripe) are another option. Fares vary from HK$1.50 to HK$20. Exact change is needed for minibuses and you pay as you get on. With maxicabs, you pay as you get out and the drivers can usually offer small change. Again, drivers do not speak much English.

There are large bus terminals beside the Central Ferry Piers and Admiralty MTR station, beneath Exchange Square and in front of the Star Ferry Concourse in Tsim Sha Tsui. You can pick up free maps of major bus routes at HKTA Information and Gift Centres or call the bus company hotlines listed above.

Trams

There are two types of trams on Hong Kong Island.

The Peak Tram – which is really a funicular railway – has been scaling the heights of Victoria Peak for more than 100 years. The lower terminus is on Garden Road (and is served by a free open-top shuttle bus from the City Hall (east) side of the Star Ferry concourse in Central). It runs daily, every 10 to 15 minutes, from 7am to midnight. The adult fare is HK$18 one-way or HK$28 return; HK$5 one-way or HK$8 return for children under 12. For further information, call Peak Tramways, tel: 2849 7654; 2522 0922.

A fleet of 160 double-decker electric trams trundles along 14km (9 miles) of track on the north side of Hong Kong Island from Kennedy Town in the west to Shau Kei Wan in the east, with frequent stops along the way in Western, Central, Wan Chai, Happy Valley and Causeway Bay. A ride on a tram is to experience a slice of Hong Kong history as they've been plying the west-east island route since 1904, and the fleet's exterior design dates from 1925. The trams offer unrivalled value for money and a great sightseeing opportunity if you avoid rush hours and lunch-time. Enter the tram at the rear door and exit from the front. The fare is HK$2 (HK$1 for under-12s) which you drop in the box next to the driver as you leave (no change is given). The trams operate daily 6am–1am. For enquiries call Hong Kong Tramways, tel: 2559 8918.

The fleet includes two vintage 'Victorian' trams which are used for Open Top Tram Tours (HK$180 per adult/HK$140 for under-12s). Trams can also be hired for private charter (HK$570 for ordinary trams; HK$900 per hour for vintage trams; minimum charter 2 hours). For tram tour and charter bookings, contact MP Tours, tel: 2118 6243 or visit their office on 1st Floor (inside) Star Ferry Pier, Tsim Sha Tsui.

LRT (Light Rail Transit)

Only tourists travelling to the western New Territories will use the Light Rail, which runs between Tuen Mun ferry pier and Yuen Long from 5.40am to 12.30am daily. Fares range from HK$4 to HK$5.80 (HK$2–2.90 for children under 12). LRT hotline, tel: 2468 7788.

Disabled Travellers' Access

With the exception of Chek Lap Kok International Airport, major hotels and some of the newer public and commercial buildings, Hong Kong is not an easy place for physically or visually challenged travellers to navigate. Two useful publications to consult are HKTA's free *Access Guide for Disabled Visitors* (available from HKTA Information and Gift Centres) and the Transport Department's *Guide to Public Transport Services in Hong Kong for Disabled Persons* (available from the Transport Department, 41st Floor, Immigration Tower, Gloucester Road, Wan Chai; tel: 2829 5223).

Limousines

Hong Kong has more Rolls-Royces per head than any other city. But the most common limo for hire is the ubiquitous Mercedes Benz. Ace Hire Car Service, 16 Min Fat Street, Happy Valley; tel: 2893 0541, charges HK$160 per hour for a 4-seater Mercedes and HK$250 per hour for a 7-seater stretch-limousine, inclusive of driver but exclusive of tunnel fees.

Rental Cars

With one of the world's best public transportation networks, there's hardly reason to rent a car in Hong Kong. But if the need arises, expect to pay from HK$800 per day for a small economy car like a Honda Civic, with a cash or credit card deposit of HK$10,000. To rent a car in Hong Kong you must be over 25 and have held an overseas or international driving licence for at least 2 years. You need to produce your driving licence and passport at time of rental. Avis Rent-A-Car is at Ground Floor, Bright Star Mansion, 93 Leighton Road, Causeway Bay, tel: 2890 6988.

Helicopters

If you've got the bucks, one of the most spectacular ways to see Hong Kong is by helicopter. Heliservices (tel: 2802 0200) offer chartered aerial tours of Hong Kong SAR, leaving from the Central Helipad on Hong Kong Island, from HK$4,750 for 30 minutes or HK$9,500 for one hour. East Asia Airlines (tel: 2859 3359) will fly you by helicopter to Macau in 18 minutes for HK$1,206 on weekdays, HK$1,310 at weekends. Return flights are double one way less one dollar! (booking office 3F Shun Tak Centre/Macau Ferry Pier).

Boat Tours & Charters

Watertours of HK Ltd (tel: 2739 3302) offer 8 different water or land tours. Regular cruises include Morning Harbour & Noon Day Gun Firing (10.15am daily) and Western Harbour & Tsing Ma Bridge (2.45pm daily), with pick-up from Kowloon Public Pier in Tsim Sha Tsui and 15 minutes later from Queen's Pier in Central (HK$200 for adults, HK$110 for under-12s); Aberdeen & Harbour Night Cruise, with pick-up from selected hotels (HK$590 for adults, HK$490 for under-12s, including drinks on board and dinner at one of the floating Chinese restaurants). Tickets can be bought from Shop B17, Basement, Star House, Tsim Sha Tsui; or from the refreshment kiosk at Queen's Pier in Central.

MP Tours Ltd (tel: 2118 6243) offer daily Star Ferry cruises around Victoria Harbour, with pick-up from Star Ferry piers in Tsim Sha Tsui and (10 minutes later) in Central (5 cruises daily; duration around 1 hour; HK$180 for adults, HK$140 for under-12s). Alternatively, they can arrange private charter of a Star Ferry for HK$1,400 per hour mid-week/HK$2,000 per hour on weekend/holidays. Bookings can be made by phone or in person at their office on 1st Floor (inside) Star Ferry Pier, Tsim Sha Tsui.

The Pearl River Delta and waters off Lantau island are home to a unique and endangered group of remarkable bright pink-coloured Chinese White Dolphin (*Sousa chinensis*). Hong Kong Dolphinwatch offer regular half-day (HK$280 for adults, HK$140 for under-12s) and full-day boats trips (HK$350 for adults, HK$175 for under-12s, inclusive of buffet lunch) through the scenic western harbour to the dolphins' favourite waters. For enquiries contact Hong Kong Dolphinwatch, tel: 2984 1414; e-mail: dolphins@hk.super.net; Homepage: http://www.zianet.com/dolphins.

You can also charter your own 53-footer Chinese pleasure junk complete with 2 crew members from Simpson Marine in Aberdeen (tel: 2555 7349; e-mail: simpsonm@netvigator.com) starting at HK$2,500 for an evening or weekday and HK$5,500 for Sunday or holidays.

More informal sampan rides can be had by negotiating with the sampan operators in the typhoon shelters at Aberdeen, Sai Kung and Cheung Chau harbours.

Rickshaws

The days when rickshaws were a bonafide method of transport are long gone. A few frail, old rickshaw 'drivers' still linger around Star Ferry in Central; but these days they derive their income by posing for photographs and occasionally taking the odd naive tourist for an expensive ride round the block. Negotiate a price before taking any photos.

Maps

In addition to HKTA's basic tourist map, *The Official Hong Kong Map*, city walking tours and free leaflets containing maps of nature trails and country parks, including *Five Walks*, *Nature Walks* and *Coastal Walks* and a *Green Guide to Hong Kong*, are available from HKTA Information and Gift Centres (see *Tourist Information* on page 101).

Maps and booklets on Hong Kong's country parks are on sale at the Government Publications Centre, Ground Floor, Lower Block, Queensway Government Offices, 66 Queensway, Admiralty (tel: 2537 1910; open Monday to Friday 9am–6pm; Saturday 9am–1pm).

Friends of the Earth (FoE) publish a series of coastal guides containing pull-out walking maps packed with information on Hong Kong's rich coastal heritage. Titles include *Hong Kong Island and Po Toi Island*, *Lamma Island* and *Lantau Island*; and are available from HKTA Information and Gift Centres and

FoE's office at 2nd Floor, 53–55 Lockhart Road, Wan Chai, tel: 2528 5588.

If you're staying for a few weeks or more, you might also want to invest in the bilingual A–Z style *Hong Kong Guidebook* (Universal Publications, updated yearly, HK$62) on sale at HKTA Information and Gift Centres and most bookshops. It's usually packaged with a free *Public Transport Boarding Guide* (very useful if you plan to do much travel by public transport).

HOURS & HOLIDAYS

Business Hours

Offices generally open 9am–5pm Monday through Friday, but some government offices open at 8.30am and close at 4.30pm; many commercial offices also work a half day (9am–1pm) on Saturday.

The banks are open from 9am to 4.30pm on weekdays and from 9am to 12.30pm on Saturdays.

Most shops and stores do not get going until around 10am. They tend to stay open until 6–7pm in Central; and until 9–9.30pm in Causeway Bay, Wan Chai, Mong Kok, Tsim Sha Tsui as well as Yau Ma Tei.

Some shops in prime tourist areas like Tsim Sha Tsui stay open till late, until 10–11pm. Many shops open seven days a week all year round except during Chinese New Year.

Public Holidays

Hong Kong's public holidays embrace a happy mixture of Chinese, Christian and political feast days.

You can expect banks, government offices, post offices, schools, service organisations and some shops to be closed on the following days:

Every Sunday
New Year's Day: January 1
Lunar New Year: three days in late January/February
Good Friday: March or April
Saturday following Good Friday: March or April
Easter Monday: March or April
Ching Ming Festival: April
Labour Day: May 1
Buddha's Birthday: May
Tuen Ng (Dragon Boat) Festival: June
Hong Kong Special Administratvie Region Establishment Day: July 1
Day following Mid-Autumn Festival: September
China National Day: October 1
Chung Yeung Festival: October
Christmas Day: December 25
First weekday after Christmas Day: December

If a festival falls on a Sunday or two festivals coincide, the day preceding or following the festival is usually designated as a general holiday.

ACCOMMODATION

Hong Kong hotels are both famous and notorious. Famous in that top-flight hotels like the Mandarin, Peninsula and Regent are consistently voted among the world's best in terms of service, facilities and cuisine. Notorious in that you pay more for these fineries than just about anywhere else in Asia. However, recently tourists have benefited from a new mood of realism that set in with the Asian economic crisis of 1998, and many Hong Kong hotels are offering 'value-added' packages or discounts (of up to 60 percent in some cases) on published 'rack' rates. It's definitely worthwhile doing some advance research through travel agents or the Internet. The Hong Kong Tourist Association's Website is a good place to start (see *Tourist Information*). Published prices for a standard double are categorised as follows:

$	=	under HK$500
$$	=	HK$500–800
$$$	=	HK$801–1,200
$$$$	=	HK$1,201–2,000
$$$$$	=	HK$2,001–2,500
$$$$$$	=	above HK$2,500

Add 10 percent service charge and 3 percent government tax to all rates unless otherwise stated. While there may be significant savings to be made through special deals, the hotels' full published rates are a good indicator of the level of comfort or facilities on offer.

Airport

REGAL AIRPORT HOTEL
9 Cheong Tat Road, Chek Lap Kok
Tel: 2286 8888 Fax: 2286 8686
1,100 rooms. Hong Kong's largest hotel tucked in beside the world's largest airport. Ten restaurants and a landscaped garden and pool round off an efficient and well-equipped package. $$$$$

Hong Kong Island

CONRAD INTERNATIONAL HONG KONG
Pacific Place II, 88 Queensway, Admiralty (Conrad)
Tel: 2521 3838 Fax: 2521 3888
513 rooms. A European-style deluxe boutique hotel. Understated elegance; spacious rooms and good location adjacent to Pacific Place shopping, Hong Kong Park, Admiralty MTR and tramlines. $$$$$$

GRAND HYATT HONG KONG
1 Harbour Road, Wan Chai
Tel: 2588 1234 Fax: 2802 0677
572 rooms. Probably the most expensive and glitziest hotel in Hong Kong. Luxury on a truly palatial level; overlooking the harbour and only a couple of steps from the HK Convention and Exhibition Centre, the HK Arts Centre. $$$$$$

MANDARIN ORIENTAL HONG KONG
5 Connaught Road, Central
Tel: 2522 0111 Fax: 2810 6190
542 rooms. Classy hotel established in 1963 and consistently rated among the world's best. Impeccable service and quality. Full range of facilities including a indoor pool and some of the finest hotel F&B establishments in town. Convenient location in heart of Central. $$$$$$

THE RITZ-CARLTON HONG KONG
3 Connaught Road, Central
Tel: 2877 6666 Fax: 2877 6778
216 rooms. Post-modernist exterior gives way to classy traditionalist interior decorated with period art and antiques. Facilities include outdoor pool and good Italian and Japanese restaurants. Convenient location close to Central MTR, Star Ferry, and Admiralty and Central business and commercial districts. $$$$$$

HOTEL FURAMA HONG KONG
1 Connaught Road, Central
Tel: 2525 5111 Fax: 2845 9339
516 rooms. Quietly plush business hotel. Good value considering its convenient location to Central MTR, Star Ferry, and Admiralty and the Central district. $$$$$

ISLAND SHANGRI-LA HONGKONG
Pacific Place, Supreme Court Road Queensway (Island Shangri-La)
Tel: 2877 3838 Fax: 2521 8742
565 rooms. This gracious oasis lives up to its name. Elegant decor, helpful staff and beautiful, spacious rooms with stunning panoramic views of the harbour or The Peak. Great location; adjacent to Hong Kong Park, Pacific Place shopping and Admiralty MTR and tramlines. $$$$$

THE EXCELSIOR
281 Gloucester Road, Causeway Bay
Tel: 2894 8888 Fax: 2895 6459
897 rooms; 600 with side/full harbour view overlooking the colourful Causeway Bay typhoon shelter. Managed by the Mandarin Oriental Hotel Group, the hotel offers efficient service and a pleasant environment. Close to Causeway Bay's shopping and commercial district and MTR. $$$$$

CENTURY HONG KONG HOTEL
238 Jaffe Road, Wan Chai
Tel: 2598 8888 Fax: 2598 8866
516 rooms. Modern hotel with good facilities including an outdoor pool, health-club and Lao Ching Hing, one of the best Shanghainese restaurants in town. Convenient for HK Exhibition and Convention Centre and Wan Chai's commercial district. $$$$

RENAISSANCE HARBOUR VIEW
1 Harbour Road, Wan Chai
Tel: 2802 8888 Fax: 2802 8833
862 rooms. A shade cheaper than the Grand Hyatt but enjoys same prime location overlooking the harbour; with easy access to Kowloon from Wan Chai Ferry Pier. Superb recreational facilities. $$$$

THE EMPEROR (HAPPY VALLEY) HOTEL
1A Wang Tak Street, Happy Valley

Tel: 2893 3693 Fax: 2834 6777
158 rooms. Boutique hotel in peaceful location near Happy Valley racecourse, only minutes away from Causeway Bay. Courtesy shuttle bus to major business districts on Hong Kong Island. Pays special attention to the needs of women travellers. $$$$

THE SOUTH CHINA HOTEL
67–75 Java Road, North Point
Tel: 2503 1168 Fax: 2512 8698
204 rooms. Well-appointed with modern decor and facilities. Cantonese restaurant. Close to North Point MTR and ferry piers. $$$$

THE WHARNEY HOTEL
57–73 Lockhart Road, Wan Chai
Tel: 2861 1000 Fax: 2865 6023
335 rooms. Smart modern hotel with good facilities including indoor pool. Located in the heart of Wan Chai's commercial and nightlife district, close to HK Convention and Exhibition Centre, MTR and trams. $$$$

CENTURY HARBOUR HOTEL
508 Queen's Road West, Western
Tel: 2974 1234 Fax: 2213 6642
282 rooms. New hotel in the middle of the very traditional Western district. Courtesy shuttle bus transfers to MTR and Airport Express in Central. Excellent value for money. $$$

GRAND PLAZA
2 Kornhill Road, Quarry Bay
Tel: 2886 0011 Fax: 2886 1738
248 rooms. Modern business hotel with good facilities including golf putting green, tennis courts, indoor pool and gym. Close to Tai Koo MTR. $$$

HARBOUR VIEW INTERNATIONAL HOUSE
4 Harbour Road, Wan Chai
Tel: 2802 0111 Fax: 2802 9063
320 rooms. Worth paying the extra HK$200 for a harbour view room but book early at this upscale YMCA, next door to Hong Kong Arts Centre and directly across from the Hong Kong Convention and Exhibition Centre. $$$ (tax exempt)

HOTEL NEW HARBOUR
41–49 Hennessy Road, Wan Chai
Tel: 2861 1166 Fax: 2865 6111
173 rooms. One of the cheapest deals for a centrally-located hotel on Hong Kong Island. Convenient for HK Convention and Exhibition Centre, Wan Chai's commercial and entertainment districts, MTR and tramlines. $$$

NEW CATHAY HOTEL
17 Tung Lo Wan Road, Causeway Bay
Tel: 2577 8211 Fax: 2576 9365
225 rooms. Good option for lone travellers with singles from HK$650. Close to tramlines, Hong Kong Stadium, Victoria Park and Causeway Bay commercial, dining and shopping districts. $$$

MA WUI HALL YOUTH HOSTEL
Mount Davis Path, Victoria Road
Tel: 2788 1638 (map and info); 2817 5715
112 dormitory beds and 3 family rooms. Spartan accommodation but superb views from mountain top location above Kennedy Town and Pokfulam. Popular and hard to beat at HK$65. Book ahead through the Hong Kong Youth Hostel Association (check if your home country YHA membership is valid or whether you need to join the HKYHA; HK$180 per year). $

Kowloon

THE PENINSULA HONG KONG
Salisbury Road, Tsim Sha Tsui
Tel: 2920 2888 Fax: 2722 4170
300 rooms. Hong Kong's oldest and most prestigious hotel has been a byword for impeccable service and colonial-style grandeur since it opened in 1928. Extensively refurbished, with a new 30-storey extension tower. Eight top restaurants and superb location in the heart of Kowloon's shopping, restaurant and entertainment area; close to Tsim Sha Tsui MTR. $$$$$$

THE REGENT HONG KONG
18 Salisbury Road, Tsim Sha Tsui
Tel: 2721 1211 Fax: 2739 4546
602 rooms. Elegant with breathtaking views across Victoria Harbour. The luxu-

rious facilities you would expect of a Four Seasons hotel, including a poolside spa and 7 top restaurants. Superb location on the waterfront; convenient for Star Ferry and Kowloon's prime commercial and entertainment district. $$$$$$

KOWLOON SHANGRI-LA HOTEL
64 Mody Road, Tsim Sha Tsui East
Tel: 2721 2111 Fax: 2723 8686
719 rooms. Opulent grandeur and great harbour views. Full range of deluxe facilities including indoor swimming pool and highly rated restaurants. Across from Tsim Sha Tsui East waterfront with easy hoverferry access to Central. $$$$$

SHERATON HONG KONG HOTEL AND TOWERS
20 Nathan Road, Tsim Sha Tsui
Tel: 2369 1111 Fax: 2739 8707
798 rooms. Swish hotel on corner of Nathan and Salisbury roads with full range of deluxe facilities including an outdoor pool and 5 top-notch restaurants. Good location close to museums, MTR, and Kowloon's prime commercial and entertainment district. $$$$$

THE HONG KONG HOTEL
Harbour City, 3 Canton Road
Tsim Sha Tsui
Tel: 2113 0088 Fax: 2113 0011
710 rooms; many with magnificent harbour views. Deluxe facilities include an outdoor pool and 5 restaurants. Shopping opportunities are unparalled as it's inside the enormous shopping complex which stretches from Ocean Terminal up to the Gateway. $$$$$

HOTEL NIKKO HONG KONG
72 Mody Road, Tsim Sha Tsui East
Tel: 2739 1111 Fax: 2311 3122
462 rooms. Plush Japanese business hotel with impeccable service and panoramic harbour views. The hotel's amenities include an outdoor pool and good Cantonese, French and Japanese restaurants. Just across from Tsim Sha Tsui East waterfront promenade and convenient for HK Science Museum, Coliseum, Kowloon KCR station and the Cross Harbour Tunnel. $$$$

MAJESTIC
348 Nathan Road, Yau Ma Tei
Tel: 2781 1333 Fax: 2781 1773
387 rooms. Well-appointed business hotel. Close to Temple Street night market, shops, cinema and Jordan MTR; also well-served by buses. $$$$

THE KOWLOON HOTEL
19–21 Nathan Road, Tsim Sha Tsui
Tel: 2369 8698 Fax: 2739 9811
736 rooms. Smart, modern business hotel tucked in behind 'The Pen', in the heart of Kowloon's prime commercial and entertainment district. Close to MTR. $$$$

THE MARCO POLO HONG KONG
Harbour City, 13 Canton Road,
Tsim Sha Tsui
Tel: 2113 0888 Fax: 2113 0022
438 rooms. Elegant, Continental-style hotel in the middle of enormous Harbour City complex; marginally cheaper than sister-hotel the Hong Kong Hotel but lacking the views and the pool. $$$$

THE PRINCE HONG KONG
Harbour City, 23 Canton Road,
Tsim Sha Tsui
Tel: 2113 1888 Fax: 2113 0066
402 rooms. Similar standard to sister-hotel the Marco Polo; with outdoor pool. Very convenient for China Ferry Terminal and Kowloon Park. $$$$

BP INTERNATIONAL HOUSE
8 Austin Road, Kowloon
Tel: 2376 1111 Fax: 2376 1333
535 rooms. Marvellous location – in the heart of Tsim Sha Tsui yet separated from it by Kowloon Park. Rooms are nothing special but perfectly adequate. $$$

EATON HOTEL HONG KONG
380 Nathan Road, Yau Ma Tei
Tel: 2782 1818 Fax: 2782 5563
466 rooms. Well-equipped rooms; good value restaurants with regular clientele. Close to Temple Street night market, shops, cinema and Jordan MTR. $$$

HOTEL CONCOURSE
22 Lai Chi Kok Road, Mong Kok
Tel: 2397 6683 Fax: 2381 3768

430 rooms. Well-appointed modern hotel popular with Asian business travellers. Bargain shopping nearby in Fa Yuen Street factory-outlets. Close to Prince Edward MTR. $$$

NATHAN HOTEL
378 Nathan Road, Yau Ma Tei
Tel: 2388 5141 Fax: 2770 4262
186 rooms. Close to Temple Street night market, Jordan MTR, restaurants, shops and cinemas. $$$

THE IMPERIAL HOTEL HONG KONG
30–34 Nathan Road, Tsim Sha Tsui
Tel: 2366 2201 Fax: 2311 2360
222 rooms. Pleasant rooms. Good value; at the bottom end of this price category. Convenient location on Tsim Sha Tsui's 'Golden Mile', close to shops, restaurants, MTR and Kowloon Park. $$$

EVERGREEN HOTEL
42–52 Woo Sung Street, Yau Ma Tei
Tel: 2780 4222 Fax: 2385 8584
68 rooms. Clean tidy rooms. Triples and 4-bed rooms are good value for small groups. Steps from Temple Street night market and Jordan MTR. $$

'THE SALISBURY' (YMCA)
41 Salisbury Road, Tsim Sha Tsui
Tel: 2369 2211 Fax: 2739 9315
366 rooms. Book ahead to be sure of a room at this very upscale YMCA. All rooms are well-equipped and many enjoy panoramic views of the harbour. Amenities include a large indoor pool and an impressive range of sports facilities. As conveniently located as 'The Pen'; but at a fraction of the cost. $$ (tax exempted)

ANNE BLACK GUEST HOUSE (YWCA)
5 Man Fuk Road, Ho Man Tin
Tel: 2713 9211 Fax: 2761 1269
169 rooms. Clean, simple rooms for women and couples. A short walk away from the Ladies' Market, Mong Kok KCR and MTR stations. $ (tax exempt)

CARITAS BIANCHI LODGE
4 Cliff Road, Yau Ma Tei
Tel: 2388 1111 Fax: 2770 6669
90 rooms. Clean, spacious rooms in well-run Roman Catholic hostel between Nathan Road and the Meteorological Station. Close to Temple Street night market, shops, restaurants, and Yau Ma Tei MTR. $ (tax exempted)

CHUNGKING HOUSE
4–5 Floors, Block A, Chungking Mansions, 40 Nathan Road, Tsim Sha Tsui
Tel: 2366 5362 Fax: 2721 3570
75 rooms. There are cheaper deals in the area but Chungking House is the only establishment to win the HKTA's seal of approval. Located on Kowloon's 'Golden Mile'. Steps away from MTR. $

HEALTH & EMERGENCIES

Hotlines

Emergency: 999 (for police, fire or ambulance)
Samaritans: 2896 0000
Social Welfare Hotline: 2343 2255
Tropical Cyclone Warning: 2835 1473
Community Advice Bureau: 2815 5444

Hospitals

Queen Mary Hospital: 102 Pokfulam Road, Pokfulam, Hong Kong Island; tel: 2855 4111 (switchboard); 2855 3111 (emergencies).
Queen Elizabeth Hospital: 30 Gascoigne Road, Kowloon; tel: 2958 8888.
Prince of Wales Hospital: 30 32 Ngan Shing Street, Shatin, New Territories; tel: 2632 2211.
Adventist Hospital: No 40 Stubbs Road Happy Valley, Hong Kong Island; tel: 2574 6211.

General Practitioners

Anderson & Partners: 501 Prince's Building, Central; tel: 2523 8166 (24 hrs), and 6th Floor, Pacific Centre, 28 Hankow Road, Tsim Sha Tsui, Kowloon; tel: 2367 3011.
Central Medical Practice: 1501 Prince's Building, Central; tel: 2521 2567.

Dental Clinics

Drs Costello & Associates: 19th Floor, Coda Plaza, 51 Garden Road, Central; tel: 2877 9622.

Bayley & Jackson Dental Surgeons: Room 1502, Chekiang First Bank Centre,1 Duddell Street, Central; tel: 2526 1061.

Medications and Innoculations

A wide range of medications, including anti-malaria pills, can be obtained from pharmacist dispensaries in larger branches of Watson's.

For cholera, typhoid, hepatitis and other injections, and prescription medications not available at Watson's, try one of the GP's surgeries listed above; but be prepared to pay a consultation fee of HK$420 exclusive medication. If you're prepared to queue, basic prescriptions and medical treatments can be obtained cheaply from the numerous local government clinics throughout the territory.

Hygiene and Toilet Facilities

The main health hazard tourists are likely to encounter in Hong Kong comes from locally-caught seafood; especially shellfish, which carries a risk of food-poisoning and Hepatitis A due to Hong Kong's badly polluted waters.

A sensible precaution is to avoid locally-caught shellfish (many establishments offer fresh seafood flown in from Australia and other countries; if in doubt, ask). It is a good idea to receive Hepatitis A and B vaccinations before you leave home country.

Water direct from the government mains meets World Health Organisation standards; bottled water is also widely available here.

Toilets are mostly Western style but you still come across squat toilets in older restaurants and public toilets in rural areas. At restaurants located in shopping malls and office-blocks, you may need to ask for a key to gain access to the toilet. It's a good idea to carry a packet of tissues as toilet paper is often scarce.

Police Emergencies

Members of the Hong Kong Police Force wear navy blue uniforms in winter and olive green uniforms in summer. Many police officers speak English and are generally helpful.

The police headquarters is located at Arsenal Street in Wan Chai; there are police stations and reporting centres throughout the territory including in the Airport Express section of Hong Kong station in Central.

In an emergency dial tel: 999. To report crimes or make complaints against taxi drivers call Hong Kong's Crime Hotline at tel: 2527 7177.

For the Japanese-speaking tourists, the police hotline is tel: 2529 0000.

COMMUNICATIONS & NEWS

Post and Telecommunications

Most post offices in Hong Kong are open Monday to Saturday 8am–6pm, and Sunday and some public holidays 8am–2pm.

The best places to dispatch packages and registered items are the General Post Office next to the Star Ferry Terminal in Central and the large post office on the ground floor of Hermes House, 10 Middle Road, Tsim Sha Tsui, Kowloon. For enquiries, call tel: 2921 2222.

Public telephones can be found all around Hong Kong, but the easiest places to find them are in MTR stations, 7-Eleven stores and hotel lobbies. Local calls are free, except for a HK$1 per five minutes charge at public coin/phonecard and credit card phones; hotels often levy a charge on calls made from your room.

You can make international direct dial (IDD) calls from public card phones with a stored-value phone card (available at HKTA Information and Gift Centres, 7-Eleven stores and some bookshops).

You can also make IDD calls from sound-proof booths and send faxes at the following Cable & Wireless HKT Service Centres: 161 Des Voeux Road, Central, tel: 2534 0603; 147 Johnston Road, Wan Chai, tel: 2892 1997; Basement, London Plaza, 219 Nathan Road, Jordan, tel: 2710 6633 (open Monday to Saturday 10am–7pm; closed Sunday and holidays); and Ground Floor, Hermes House, 10 Middle Road, Tsim Sha Tsui, tel: 2724 8322/2888 7185 (24 hours daily). The service centres operate on a cash or stored-value phonecard basis only; credit cards and cheques are not accepted.

Useful Telephone Numbers

Hong Kong Directory Inquiries: 1081
Hongkong Telecom Information and Customer Service: 1000
International Directory and Customer Service: 10013
International Operator/Collect calls: 10010
Time & Temperature: 18501
International Direct Dial: Dial the access code 001, followed by the country code.

News & Media

Hong Kong has four terrestial television stations: ATV World and TVB Pearl broadcast in English; ATV Home and TVB Jade in Cantonese. The vast majority of programmes on the English-language stations are American network shows and movies. Very few English language shows are produced locally except for news and public affairs programmes. Most hotels are plugged into the Star TV satellite system and/or the Cable TV subscription system which offer a mixed bag of news, documentaries and current affairs, sports, music and drama. (CNN, BBC World, Discovery, ESPN, National Geographic and TNT Cartoon Network on Cable).

Radio has improved by leaps and bounds in the last couple of years. You can tune in to 24-hours news on the BBC-World Service (675 kHz) or local Metro Plus (1044 kHz AM). For classical music, tune to RTHK Radio 4 (97.6 to 98.9 mHz); easy-listening at RTHK Radio 3 (567 and 1584 kHz/97.9 and 106.8 mHz) and 104 FM Select (104 mHz, plus 102.4 to 106.3 mHz FM). For round-the-clock contemporary music try Quote AM (864 kHz AM).

South China Morning Post dominates the English-language newspaper readership; it takes a lot of knocks from critics, but does a fair job of covering local events and is usually crammed with international wire copy and sports news. Far behind in circulation is *The Hong Kong Standard.* For a broader outlook on world events, try the *Financial Times, International Herald Tribune* and the *Asian Wall Street Journal* which are available at most newspaper stands, English-language bookstores and hotel kiosks; *USA Today International* is also printed in Hong Kong. Hotel bookstores usually have a good selection of international newspapers, as do the newspaper vendors at Star Ferry and various branches of Bookazine and Dymocks bookshops.

Hundreds of magazines are published in Hong Kong. The most useful for tourists are two freebie entertainment magazines *HK Magazine* (weekly) and *BC Magazine* (monthly). They have reviews and listings of music, movies, restaurants, nightclubs and more. Available at selected restaurants, bars, bookstores and entertainment venues around town.

Bookshops

The most comprehensive selections of English-language books and magazines in Central, Hong Kong-side, are found at **Bookazine** (Alexandra House, Hutchison House, Jardine House, Prince's Building), **Dymocks** (International Finance Centre, Star Ferry Concourse), **Hong Kong Book Centre** (25 Des Voeux Road, Exchange Square, The Landmark). **Page One** (new Harbour City extension; also in Times Square, Causeway Bay) and **Swindon** (Kowloon Star Ferry Concourse, Lock Road, Ocean Terminal) offer the most comprehensive selections in Tsim Sha Tsui. **Tai Yip** (72 Wellington Street, Central) has a good selection on Chinese art. The **Government Publications Centre** in Queensway (see *Maps*) stocks a range of government publications on Hong Kong-related subjects from guides to local flora and fauna through to offical reports.

USEFUL ADDRESSES

Tourist Information

The Hong Kong Tourist Association (HKTA) is one of the world's most efficient national tourist boards. The first thing you should do on arrival is pick up an HKTA information bag in the baggage claim area at the airport, which contains a map, current events magazine, brochures and details of day and half-day tours organised by HKTA. The HKTA Information and Gift Centre at Chek Lap Kok is located in the Buffer Halls and Transfer Areas (open daily 6am–midnight).

The HKTA has two information centres in town: Star Ferry Concourse, Tsim Sha Tsui, Kowloon (open Monday to Friday 8am–6pm; weekends and public holidays 9am–5pm) and Shop 8, Basement, Jardine House, 1 Connaught Place, Central, Hong Kong Island (open Monday to Friday 9am–6pm; and Saturday 9am–1pm).

HKTA operates a multilingual Visitor Hotline, tel: (852) 2508 1234 (Monday to Friday 8am–6pm; weekends and holidays 9am–5pm local Hong Kong time); a world-wide English-language facsimile information retrieval service (set your fax to polling mode, then dial (852) 900 6077 1128 for the information menu; and an award-winning Website at <http://www.hkta.org>.

Consulates & Visa Offices

Australia: 24th Floor, Harbour Centre, 25 Harbour Road, Wan Chai; tel: 2827 8881.

Austria: 22nd Floor, Chinachem Tower, 34–37 Connaught Road, Central; tel: 2522 8086.

Belgium: 9th Floor, St John's Bldg, 33 Garden Road, Central; tel: 2524 3111.

Canada: 12th Floor, Tower One, Exchange Square, 8 Connaught Place, Central; tel: 2810 4321.

China (People's Republic): visa applications c/o branches of China Travel Services (CTS) and the head office at CTS House, 78 Connaught Road, Central; tel: 2853 3888. (Express visas for travel in mainland China cost HK$210; ordinary service HK$160.) For non-travel related enquiries, contact the Consulate Department, Office of the Commissioner of the Ministry of Foreign Affairs, 5th Floor, Lower Block, China Resources Building, 26 Harbour Road, Wan Chai; tel: 2585 1794, 2827 1881.

Denmark: 24th Floor, Great Eagle Centre, 23 Harbour Road, Wan Chai; tel: 2827 8101.

Finland: 18th Floor, Hutchison House, 10 Harcourt Road, Central; tel: 2525 5385.

France: 26th Floor, Tower Two, Admiralty Centre, 18 Harcourt Road, Central; tel: 2529 4351.

Germany: 21st Floor, United Centre, 95 Queensway, Admiralty; tel: 2529 8855.

Greece: 25th Floor, Pacific Place Tower Two, 88 Queensway, Admiralty; tel: 2774 1682.

India: Unit D, 16F, United Centre, 95 Queensway. Admiralty; tel: 2528 4028.

Israel: 7th Floor, Tower Two, Admiralty Centre, 18 Harcourt Road, Central; tel: 2529 6091.

Italy: 8th Floor, Hutchison House, 10 Harcourt Road, Central; tel: 2522 0033.

Japan: 46th Floor, Tower One, Exchange Square, Central; tel: 2522 1184.

Korea (South): 5th Floor, Far East Finance Centre, 16 Harcourt Road, Central; tel: 2529 4141.

Malaysia: 24F, Malaysia Bldg, 50 Gloucester Road, Central; tel: 2527 0921.

Netherlands: 3rd Floor, China Bldg, 29 Queen's Road, Central; tel: 2522 5127.

New Zealand: 65th Floor, Central Plaza, 18 Harbour Road, Wan Chai; tel: 2877 4488.

Norway: 15th Floor, Great Eagle Centre, 23 Harbour Road, Wan Chai; tel: 2587 9953.

Portugal: 9th Floor, Harbour Centre, Harbour Road, Wan Chai; tel: 2802 2586.

Singapore: 9th Floor, Tower One, Admiralty Centre, 18 Harcourt Road, Admiralty; tel: 2527 2212.

South Africa: 27th Floor, Great Eagle Centre, 23 Harbour Road, Wan Chai; tel: 2577 3279.

Spain: 8th Floor, Printing House, 18 Ice House Street, Central; tel: 2525 3041.

Sweden: 8th Floor, Hong Kong Club Bldg, 3A Chater Road, Central; tel: 2521 1212.

Switzerland: 37th Floor, Gloucester Tower, The Landmark, 11 Pedder Street, Central; tel: 2522 7147.

Taiwan (Republic of China): visa applications c/o Chung Hwa Travel, 4th Floor, Lippo Tower, Lippo Centre, 89 Queensway, Admiralty; tel: 2525 8315.

Thailand: 8th Floor, Fairmont House, 8 Cotton Tree Drive, Central; tel: 2521 6481.

United Kingdom: c/o The British Consulate General, 1 Supreme Court Road; tel: 2901 3000/3111.

United States: 26 Garden Road, Central; tel: 2523 9011.

Airline Offices

Aeroflot Russian Airlines: 2nd Floor, New Henry House, 10 Ice House Street, Central; tel: 2845 4232 (res); 2769 6031 (flight info).

Air Canada: 16th Floor, Wheelock House, 20 Pedder Street, Central; tel: 2522 1001 (res); 2769 6032 (flight info).

Air France: 21st Floor, Alexandra House, 16 Chater Road, Central; tel: 2524 8145 (res); 2116 8730 (flight info).

Air New Zealand: 17th Floor, Li Po Chun Chambers, 189 Des Voeux Road, Central; tel: 2524 9041 (res); 2842 3642 (flight info).

Alitalia: 8th Floor, Vicwood Plaza, 199 Des Voeux Road, Central; tel: 2534 6998 (res & flight info); 2769 6046 (recorded flight info).

Ansett Australia: 17th Floor, Li Po Chun Chambers, 189 Des Voeux Road, Central; tel: 2527 7883 (res); 2842 3642 (flight info).

British Airways: 30th Floor, Alexandra House, 16 Chater Road, Central; tel: 2868 0303 (res); 2868 0768 (flight info).

Canadian Airlines: 16th Floor, Tower One, New World Tower, 18 Queen's Road, Central; tel: 2867 8111 (res); 2769 7113 (flight info).

Cathay Pacific: 10th Floor, The Peninsula Office Tower, 18 Middle Road, Tsim Sha Tsui; tel: 2747 1888 (res); 2747 1234 (flight info).

China National Aviation Corp (CNAC): Ground Floor, CNAC Building, 10 Queen's Road Central; tel: 2861 0322/ 2973 3733 (res); 2216 1088 (flight info).

Dragonair: 46th Floor, Cosco Tower, 183 Queen's Road Central; tel: 2590 1188 (res/flight info); 2868 6777 (general office).

Emirates Airlines: 37th Floor, Gloucester Tower, The Landmark, Central; tel: 2526 7171 (res); 2801 8700 (flight info).

Japan Airlines (JAL): 20th Floor, Gloucester Tower, The Landmark, Central; tel: 2523 0081 (res); 2769 6524 (flight info).

KLM Royal Dutch Airlines: 22nd Floor, World Trade Centre, 280 Gloucester Road, Causeway Bay; tel: 2808 2111 (res); 2769 6046 (flight info).

Lauda Air: 9th Floor, Tower Two, South Seas Centre, 75 Mody Road, Tsim Sha Tsui East; tel: 2525 5222 (res); 2180 2180 (flight info).

Lufthansa: 11th Floor, Wing Shan Tower, 173 Des Voeux Road Central, Sheung Wan; tel: 2868 2313 (res/flight info).

Northwest Airlines: 29th Floor, Alexandra House, 16 Chater Road, Central; tel: 2810 4288 (res/flight info).

Qantas Airways: 37th Floor, Jardine House, 1 Connaught Place, Central; tel: 2842 1438 (res); 2842 1400 (flight info).

Singapore Airlines: 17th Floor, United Centre, 95 Queensway, Admiralty; tel: 2520 2233 (res); 2769 6387 (flight info).

Swissair: 8th Floor, Tower Two, Admiralty Centre, 18 Harcourt Road, Central; tel: 2529 3670 (res); 2769 6387 (flight info).

Thai Airways International: 24th Floor, United Centre, 95 Queensway, Admiralty; and Shop 122–124, Worldwide Plaza, 19 Des Voeux Road Central; tel: 2876 6888 (res); 2769 7038 (flight info).

United Airlines: 29th Floor, Gloucester Tower, The Landmark, Central; tel: 2810 4888 (res); 2801 8617 (flight info).

Virgin Atlantic Airways: 27th Floor, Kinwick Centre, 32 Hollywood Road, Central; tel: 2532 6060 (res); 2180 2180 (flight info).

FURTHER READING

Fiction

Clavell, James. *Taipan*. Antheneum & Dell, New York, 1966. Rousing account of the rise of a powerful 19th-century British merchant family in Hong Kong.

Elegant, Robert. *Dynasty*. William Collins & Sons, Glasgow, 1977. The story of a powerful Eurasian family in Hong Kong from 1900 to 1970, written by a foreign correspondent based in the colony.

Feign, Larry and Nury Vittachi *The Lillygate Letters/Execute Yourself Tonight*. Hambalan, Hong Kong, 1993. A wry and extremely funny look at the 1997 issue through the eyes of the popular local cartoon heroine, Lily Wong.

Mason, Richard. *The World of Suzie Wong*. 1957, new edition Pegasus Books,

Hong Kong, 1994. The book that made Wan Chai and its bar girls famous. The tale of an English artist who falls in love with a local lass.

Yogerst, Joseph R. *White Tiger*. Mandarin, Singapore, 1992. The book is about a jaded American policeman and an ambitious British journalist tracking a serial killer in contemporary Hong Kong, against a backdrop of the impending handover to China.

Xi Xi. *Marvels of a Floating City*. Renditions Paperbacks, 1997 and *A Girl Like Me and Other Stories*. Renditions Paperbacks, enlarged edition, 1996. Two eloquent volumes of short stories from Hong Kong's foremost woman fiction writer Zhang Yan, also known as Xi Xi.

History

Endacott, G.B. *A History of Hong Kong*. Hong Kong, Oxford University Press, 1958 and 1973. Long considered 'the Bible' of Hong Kong history, this is an exhaustive study of the former British colony, from ancient to modern times.

Hong Kong Government. *Hong Kong 1998*. Meticulously detailed facts-and-figures reviewing the Hong Kong of today. Updated annually since 1946.

Hughes, Richard. *Borrowed Place, Borrowed Time*. Andre Deutsch, London, 1968 and 1976 (revised). This book by the late dean of Hong Kong's foreign correspondents takes a look at the past, present and future of the colony.

General

Insight Guide: Hong Kong. Apa Publications (HK) Ltd, Singapore, 1998 edition. Perhaps the most comprehensive guide to Hong Kong. The latest edition is packed with facts, history, culture and beautiful photographs.

Schepel, Kaarlo. *Magic Walks*. The Alternative Press, Hong Kong, 5th edition 1994. A series of descriptive area-by-area guides that takes the reader on hiking trails through Hong Kong's countryside and nature reserves.

Lloyd, Peter. *Spiritual and Alternative Hong Kong*. Pilgrims Travel Guides, 1998. A practical A–Z guide to Hong Kong's spiritual and holistic places.

Stokes, Edward. *Across Hong Kong Island* (HKCP Foundation, 1998) and *Hong Kong's Wild Places: An Environmental Exploration*. Oxford University Press, 1995. These explore the scenic beauty of Hong Kong Island and her countryside.

ACKNOWLEDGMENTS

Cover, Backcover	**Sylvain Grandadam/Apa Photo**
5, 10, 13, 14, 15B, 16, 17, 18T, 18B, 20, 22B, 24T, 25, 27B, 28B, 29T, 29B, 30T, 30B, 31, 39T, 40T, 40B, 43, 44T, 48, 49T, 49M, 49B, 58T, 59T, 59B, 60, 64B, 67T, 68, 70B, 72, 77, 78, 79T, 79B, 80B, 81T, 84T, 84B, 86T, 87T, 87B, 88TR, 88B, 94M	**Bill Wassman**
2/3, 52	**Catherine Karnow**
46	**Jon Evans**
6, 22T, 23, 24B, 27T, 28T, 32T, 32B, 33, 35T, 35B, 36T, 36B, 37T, 37B, 39B, 42, 45, 47T, 47B, 48B, 50T, 50B, 51T, 53, 54T, 54B, 55, 56, 57T, 57B, 58B, 67B, 69, 70T, 73, 74, 75, 76, 80T, 81B, 82T, 82B, 83T, 83B, 85, 86B, 88TL, 89, 93M, 93B, 94B	**Joseph R Yogerst**
Cover, 12, 20, 30, 41, 45, 48, 56, 57, 80, 81, 82, 83	**Taras Kovaliv**
61	**Alain Evrard/Apa Photo**
15	**Apa Photo Agency**
Handwriting	**V.Barl**
Cover Design	**Klaus Geisler**
Cartography	**Berndtson & Berndtson**

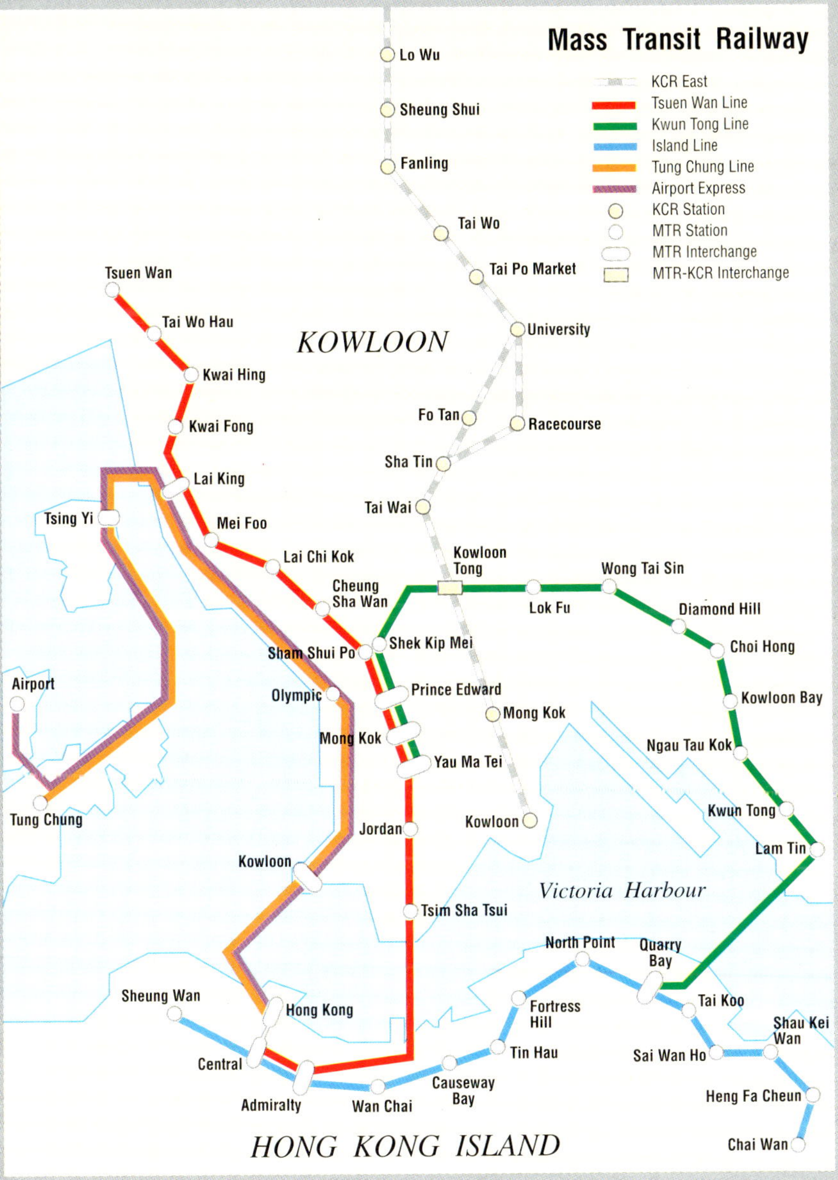

Mass Transit Railway
KCR East
Tsuen Wan Line
Kwun Tong Line
Island Line
Tung Chung Line
Airport Express
KCR Station
MTR Station
MTR Interchange
MTR-KCR Interchange
Lo Wu
Sheung Shui
Fanling
Tai Wo
Tai Po Market
University
KOWLOON
Tsuen Wan
Tai Wo Hau
Kwai Hing
Kwai Fong
Lai King
Mei Foo
Tsing Yi
Fo Tan
Racecourse
Sha Tin
Tai Wai
Lai Chi Kok
Cheung Sha Wan
Kowloon Tong
Wong Tai Sin
Lok Fu
Diamond Hill
Choi Hong
Sham Shui Po
Shek Kip Mei
Airport
Olympic
Prince Edward
Mong Kok
Kowloon Bay
Mong Kok
Yau Ma Tei
Ngau Tau Kok
Tung Chung
Jordan
Kowloon
Kwun Tong
Lam Tin
Kowloon
Victoria Harbour
Tsim Sha Tsui
North Point
Quarry Bay
Sheung Wan
Hong Kong
Fortress Hill
Tai Koo
Shau Kei Wan
Central
Tin Hau
Sai Wan Ho
Admiralty
Wan Chai
Causeway Bay
Heng Fa Cheun
Chai Wan
HONG KONG ISLAND

Index

A – B

C

D – G

H

J – K

L

M – O

P – R

S

T

U – V

W – Z